CHURCH
IN TRANSLATION

VIBRANT CHRISTIANITY IN YOUR TIME AND PLACE

DAN COLLISON
with SHELLY BARSUHN

Abingdon Press
NASHVILLE

CHURCH IN TRANSLATION
VIBRANT CHRISTIANITY IN YOUR TIME AND PLACE

Copyright © 2010 by Abingdon Press

Library of Congress Cataloging-in-Publication Data

Collison, Daniel, 1968–
    Church in translation : vibrant Christianity in your time and place / Dan Collison with Shelly Barsuhn.
        p.   cm.
    Includes bibliographical references (p.   ).
    ISBN 978-0-687-46516-3 (book - pbk./trade pbk., adhesive - perfect binding : alk. paper)
    1. Church growth.   2. Christianity and culture.   3. Church growth—United States.
4. Christianity and culture—United States.   I. Nielsen Barsuhn, Rochelle, 1958–   II. Title.
    BV652.25.C64   2010
    254'.5—dc22

                                                                        2010028221

10 11 12 13 14 15 16 17 18 19—10 9 8 7 6 5 4 3 2 1

MANUFACTURED IN THE UNITED STATES OF AMERICA

To Holly in our twentieth year

of shared journey through time and place.

You are my past, present, and future.

ACKNOWLEDGMENTS

It is impossible to pour enough gratitude on my family for the way they make me a better Christ follower. My parents give me the gift of drive. My sister gives me the gift of kindness. My brother gives me the gift of passion. My wife gives me the gift of authenticity. My boys give me the gift of play.

Friendship is often tested in the crucible of crisis and transition. I have been literally transformed by friends who were willing to journey with me over the two years leading to this book project. At the top of the list are Scott and Shelly Barsuhn. They have lavished on me the depth of love found only in families, the joy of freedom found only in friendships, and the strength of support found only in partnerships. Shelly's writing elevates every conversation it touches. Wow.

The mentors who shaped my thinking for this book are vast, and their sacrifice of time and effort on my behalf will forever inspire my gratitude. I am indebted to the faculty of Bethel Seminary, St. Paul, and the pastors of Wooddale Church in Eden Prairie, Minnesota, for framing nearly fifteen years of my thinking and experience. Most recently the Fuller Seminary doctoral program riveted me to the task of leading in the twenty-first century. Sally Morganthaler moved from being a busy author and ideation guru to mentor and friend. My pastor Wes Roberts is the kind of mentor every pastor should have: seasoned, edgy, fun, honest, loving, and rooted in the grace of our Triune God.

I am humbled to walk alongside the congregation, leaders, and staff of First Covenant Church as we reinvent church for the twenty-first century in downtown Minneapolis. The community of faith that gathers at the corner of Chicago Avenue and 7th Street is this book being lived out in real time.

I consider it an honor to partner with Abingdon Press for this project. I specifically thank Jessica Kelley for her tireless work and input. She strengthened the project from beginning to end.

CONTENTS

Contents

FOREWORD

Leading a church today is more challenging than ever. Christian leaders are asking: how do I keep my church rock-solid, built on Scripture, yet aware of the changing culture? How do I engage people who stand outside the church, who view it with disinterest and skepticism? How do I utilize the finest strengths of historic Christianity to break through to this younger generation? How do I help our members understand with their hearts, minds, souls, and strength what it will take to turn their church around?

Dan Collison is a young leader who has somehow seemed to gain fifty years of outstanding experience on the frontline of church ministry in the last twenty years. This book was forged not on ivory-tower speculation, but in the real world of change, resistance, passion, and transformation.

Each chapter will lead you to ponder one of ten critical issues that your church must consider. Reading this book will not be just an intellectual activity; it also will cause you to go to the deeper places of the Spirit, to wrestle with how your church can fulfill its God-given potential.

David Olson
Author, *The American Church in Crisis*

INTRODUCTION

The strategic plans have been distributed, the vision grid has appeared in the church annual report, and the elders have fervently worked to implement strategies that will produce megachurch growth. And yet the church is faltering. Members are quietly and steadily dropping away, and few new participants—young or old—are venturing in to take their place. Church leaders are frustrated, confused, and alarmed. They pray for revitalization, wondering, "Should we create a different kind of worship service? A novel ad campaign? More and better programs or events to draw people?"

Or have Americans just become too cynical for faith?

Accelerating technological advancement, increased access to information, dizzying economic shifts, religious and philosophical pluralism, the exponential expansion of global business, expansive social networks—these are just a few of the changes affecting the world and rippling through the church. In this highly charged atmosphere, ripe with possibility for the church to grow and minister in new ways, church attendance in America is instead decreasing.[1] Like a scratched compact disc stuttering on the same two seconds of sound over and over again, churches across America get stuck.

Scene One: A church originates from a contextual movement of people in a particular time and place—a group of people drawn together around a common mission at their unique location.

Scene Two: At some point the context surrounding the church—culture, population, business, community needs, housing—changes.

Scene Three: In response, the church changes little to nothing in its practices—falsely assuming that its past success assures future effectiveness.

Scene Four: The people surrounding the building begin to ignore the church.

Scene Five: The church loses a sense of purpose in its time and place.

Scene Six: The context ignores the church altogether and pushes it to the margins of its imagination.

Finale: The church inevitably closes its doors or hands its building off to a new church more committed to the current context.

The scenario is being played out in churches across America. Christians' most sincere efforts to reach out are falling short, and ominous statistics show that the church in America is slowly but inexorably failing. Many people have stopped looking to the church for fulfillment, meaning, and hope. They no longer believe that Christianity is a faith that will welcome and love them. They see, instead, an exclusive community. They sense they will be welcomed *if* they first clean up, fit in, and vote a particular direction. And that leaves out millions of people. Too often the church has been known for speaking out on the behavior of non-Christians rather than encouraging followers of Jesus to be like Christ, for protecting its own "rights" rather than the rights of others, and for rallying around political issues rather than wholeheartedly living out Jesus' command to serve others. The trouble is that the number of people interested in that kind of club has plummeted.

True Story

My six-year-old son has the remarkable ability to read almost anything, even if he does not fully comprehend it. Rifling through my books one afternoon, he was particularly interested in one title: *They Like Jesus but Not the Church.*[2] It was a study of current trends, seeking to answer, at least in part, why so few Americans are part of any church. Proud of his reading ability, his little mind grabbed the title and he started repeating it over and over: *"They Like Jesus but Not the Church. They Like Jesus but Not the Church."* Each time he said the title my stomach clutched. The title taunted me. Between his joyful repetitions I futilely tried to explain, "Some people *like* the church!" But my son was already creating new paraphrases: "Jesus is a genius but the church is *stupid.*" Now I was really squirming. I could just imagine him walking up to a stately member of the church and making that cheerful announcement.

Eventually he went on to other things, but my mind did not. I felt uneasy—and worried. What was the future of the church in this new reality? I imagined a book titled *They Like the Church Because Christians Live Like Jesus*, realizing that this had been the dream—and command—of Jesus in the first place. How was it possible to make such a dramatic change in the perception outsiders had of Christians? I desperately wanted to find out.

The authors of *UnChristian: What a New Generation Really Thinks about Christianity . . . and Why It Matters* paint a stark picture.

> The image of the Christian faith has suffered a major setback. Our most recent data show that young outsiders have lost much of their respect for the Christian faith. These days nearly two out of every five young outsiders (38 percent) claim to have a "bad impression of present-day Christianity." . . . This group is at least three times larger than it was just a decade ago.[3]

This is not a passive rejection.

> One of the surprising insights from our research is that the growing hostility toward Christians is very much a reflection of what outsiders feel they receive from believers. They say their aggression simply matches the oversized opinions and egos of Christians. One outsider put it this way: "Most people I meet assume that *Christian* means very conservative, entrenched in their thinking, antigay, antichoice, angry, violent, illogical empire builders; they want to convert everyone and they generally cannot live peacefully with anyone who doesn't believe what they believe."[4]

As lovers of the missional church as Jesus meant it to be, Christians must begin to acknowledge that in the face of this reality ministry grids, mission statements, and the systems of the church growth movement are inadequate. It is a new time and a new landscape. In this state of humility we must look, clear-eyed, at the transformation that has occurred in our culture—a transformation that has changed forever the way people of faith communicate with others. We must refresh our outlook even while celebrating the durability and relevance of the message of Jesus.

Imagine life and the very different practice of Christianity in the days of the early church, the Dark Ages, the Industrial Revolution, the Great Depression, or the digital age. The miracle of God's word and message is its resonance throughout time. Although every age has faced fear and resistance from believers who correlate cultural change with tampering with the core truths of Christianity, the teachings of Jesus have been mystically preserved through massive cultural transitions.

The greatest challenge for established churches in America today is to remain agile enough to continually apply the timeless message of Jesus Christ to the always-changing culture that surrounds our buildings. In other words, the church remains aware of and adaptable to its context. The church is a living entity that beautifully fits every context in every century. This "fitting in" is not pandering or caving in to culture; it is a recognition that we exist not in 1950, 1656, 1122, or 33, but right now, in a time and place that God designed.

In our postmodern—even post-Christian—Western world it is again essential that we translate God's historic truths and timeless practices. How can we tear down the cultural wall people must scale to experience Jesus? What are the essential characteristics of the twenty-first-century church? How do we reframe the elements of vibrant Christianity in today's particular context? How do we lead churches that are biblically inspired, prayer designed, intellectually informed, community formed, collaboratively led, artistically infused, mission minded, socially aware, culturally engaged, and grace filled?

This is not a special or new kind of Christianity. It is not a doctrine to memorize or a program that can be unrolled or phased in. It is a way of thinking and doing that seeps into the foundation, walls, and air of the church. It is breathed in its people—then organically breathed out. Seventh-grade science gives us a new way of thinking about this kind of church. Like the process of osmosis, through which molecules flow naturally to where they are needed, this Christianity draws people inside to experience God and community, and then out to bless their neighbors, cities, and the world through service, grace, and love.

To move forward, church leaders must make difficult and significant changes in long-held assumptions. We dare not continue "doing church" in the same way. Of course the church should foster worship, discipleship, fellowship, ministry, and evangelism—but how? With what goals? With what mind-set? A "plug and play" strategy will not work in our specific cultural landscape. To survive and create a dynamic movement toward spiritual transformation and hope in our time, the Christian church must become fully missional, understanding and speaking to its context just as Jesus understood his world and was eminently prepared to speak to its people. In that posture, the church will be able to point eloquently to Jesus the Messiah's extravagant offer: "Whoever hears my word and believes him who sent me has eternal life and will not be condemned; he has crossed over from death to life" (John 5:24).

The twenty-first-century church can do small things together to bring about great change. Growing the church will be a journey, like faith itself. It will take focus, time, and a willingness to sacrifice personal preferences. It will take the work of the spirit of God.

Jesus offers life that is expansive, not restrictive; generous, not stingy; loving, not judgmental; transformative, not comfortable. As Christians of the twenty-first century we must stand aside as God makes the words of Jesus real in the world today: "I have come that they may have life, and have it to the full" (John 10:10).

CHAPTER ONE

BIBLICALLY INSPIRED

Living the Book with Humility

> *"You diligently study the Scriptures because you think that by them you possess eternal life. These are the Scriptures that testify about me, yet you refuse to come to me to have life."*
>
> *(John 5:39-40)*

The Bible is a supernatural, mysterious, simple, complex, and beautiful message to inform and transform the lives of believers, the church, and—ultimately—culture. Christians and the church, however, have not lately been known for thoughtful handling of God's word. Rather than viewing it with awe and humility, some Christians have, in their defensiveness, reduced Scripture to a personal tool belt of judgment. Instead of grace, they have shown a penchant for using the Bible for their own purposes—quoting verses out of context, extracting Scripture to support a position on a given topic, or hijacking biblical texts to judge others' behavior. This tendency has led to a sad unraveling of the Bible's reputation as the transformative word of God. No wonder non-Christians feel attacked and embittered. No wonder churches have difficulty drawing people to God merely by asserting, "We are Bible based." To people outside the church, this statement now sounds like a door slamming shut in their faces.

But Jesus clearly delineated the correct application of Scripture, and his manner of handling God's word was instructive for believers in every century since. Today he confronts the church, reminding us that the body must be built on him, not on dogma—on insight and mercy, not on condemnation. He is asking us to understand that when we value tight philosophical systems over the genuine message of the gospel, we become a stumbling block that injures the church and wounds those we are sent to serve. In our culture and context, it is imperative that people of faith return to an understanding and practice of biblical truth as modeled by Jesus.

> One Sabbath Jesus was going through the grainfields, and as his disciples walked along, they began to pick some heads of grain. The Pharisees said to him, "Look, why are they doing what is unlawful on the Sabbath?"
>
> He answered, "Have you never read what David did when he and his companions were hungry and in need? In the days of Abiathar the high priest, he entered the house of God and ate the consecrated bread, which is lawful only for priests to eat. And he also gave some to his companions."
>
> Then he said to them, "The Sabbath was made for man, not man for the Sabbath. So the Son of Man is Lord even of the Sabbath." (Mark 2:23-28)

The day of Sabbath was originally designated by God to benefit people by setting one day a week aside for rest, community, and joy. The teachers of the law selfishly grabbed it for their own purposes and personal benefit. Adding one Sabbath law and regulation after another, they attempted to use the Sabbath day of rest as a means to direct everyone's attention and money to their religious systems and institutions. In the end everyone was forced to serve a legalistic notion of Sabbath rather than actually experience God's Sabbath rest. Jesus, using scripture, warned the Pharisees about manipulating scripture to serve them selves. Furthermore, he clarified that Scripture points to himself, the Lord of the Sabbath, and not their legalistic institutions. God's church must realign itself with this healthy, holy, and holistic view of the Bible to honor God and once again allow people to experience his word as irresistible and life changing.

Seeing the Sacredness of Scripture

Christians believe that God is the origin of Scripture. "In the beginning was the Word, and the Word was with God, and the Word was God" (John 1:1). We are told in 2 Timothy 3:16 that "all Scripture is God-breathed." Some translations of this verse use the word *inspired*, alluding to the Holy Spirit guiding a multitude of writers.

There is a mystery here. If you believe that the words in John 1:1 are inspired, what does it mean to your life, the life of the church, and the practice of faith? God *is* the word. When we approach the Bible we are approaching God—not something to be glibly done. We must view God's word on those terms and in totality, not in bits and pieces that suit our view of the world. Only by looking at Scripture in total do we approach understanding. This is a lifelong quest. The word is immense—not visible all at once. We pull back the petals one by one to find infinite layers beneath.

Christians approaching the Bible will gain insight from the art of seeing the thirty-thousand-foot view of God's word. It is only from this vantage point that we see the epic nature of the Bible. We then read the Scripture in total and apply it holistically.

Stanley Grenz, a Christian thinker of the twenty-first century, reflects:

> Our world is more than a collection of incompatible and competing local narratives. . . . We firmly believe that the local narratives of the many human communities do fit together into a single grand narrative, the story of humankind. . . . As Christians we claim to know what that grand narrative is. It is the story of God's action in history for the salvation of fallen humankind and the completion of God's intentions for creation. We boldly proclaim that the focus of this metanarrative is the story of Jesus.[1]

Not Always Literal

In a congregational meeting there was a vote to convert the historic church chapel into a gymnasium for outreach purposes. One church member stood up. "I don't see any mention of gymnasiums in the Bible." Another church member promptly responded, "I don't see any mention of urinals in the Bible either, but they sure are a good idea." The vote went in favor of transforming the chapel into a gym.

Postmodern Americans are accustomed to looking at a world of mystery. They understand incongruity, difficulty, and struggle. Faith deals with all of those elements of life. What they find hard to swallow is an insistence on the literal reading of Bible passages that are clearly meant to be understood another way. Churches hoping to speak to people in the twenty-first century must acknowledge that doggedly literal interpretations of the Bible can hold people at arm's length and keep them from the richness of the text. The Bible contains hyperbole, song, metaphor, poetry, allegory, and other forms of writing that bring God's word to life.

> By the word of the LORD were the heavens made,
>   their starry host by the breath of his mouth. . . .
> Let all the earth fear the LORD;
>   let all the people of the world revere him.
> For he spoke, and it came to be;
>   he commanded, and it stood firm. (Psalm 33:6, 8-9)

"Spoke" does not designate a literal movement of lips and tongue, of course, but is a way for us to understand and imagine in human terms and images. Rather than putting our literal selves in the way of God's message, we can read these words and faintly begin to sense the enormity of God's power. We must experience the Bible with our minds open to all that God has to say to us.

When we read the Bible thoughtfully, thoroughly, and with openness to the underlying message of the literature we avoid silliness that builds a wall between people and an encounter with God.

Reading in Context

The practice of wielding verses out of context has been devastating to the church and to the translation of Christianity into our culture. For instance, some churches have attempted to lift verses out of Paul's writings and directly apply them, without historical or cultural care, to our unique culture and time. We dare not ignore these verses' original intent and audience. Whereas the message of each biblical book is alive and vibrant, the words were originally written with a particular audience in mind. New Testament verses advising women to keep their heads covered and men to have short hair are not implemented in Christian churches today, yet we treat similar verses with strange superstition. Some churches, for example, elevate Ephesians 5:22-23 ("Wives, submit to your husbands as to the Lord. For the husband is the head of the wife.") to the level of serious dogma. They are willing to fight over this doctrine and exclude people who view these verses in light of a specific historical context. The church must wisely discern original intent, understanding the singular circumstances of Corinth, Ephesus, and Rome and avoiding the elevation of historical and cultural elements into legalistic doctrine.

In the twenty-first-century church we must return to the discipline of reading with a keen eye to everything the Bible has to say about any point of emphasis in order to avoid the improper application of isolated texts. Misreadings, misappropriations, and the extraction of verses are not new temptations. Throughout history the Bible has been inappropriately used to justify slavery, oppress women, excuse military aggression, and create theocracies. In addition to the pain these sins have caused, these misappropriations have justifiably turned people away from Jesus. Continuing in this practice will have a deadly effect. It will stunt our ability to offer hope to those around us. It is time to look hard at the practice of careless scriptural reading and application.

Proper Use of Biblical Truth

Some people read the Bible in order to gain ammunition for use against others, elevating specific passages above the generous grace of God. Henry Cloud and John Townsend describe this entanglement in their book *How People Grow*:

> Some people make the mistake of missing the One to whom the Bible is directing them. They become enamored of learning the depths and complexities of the Bible, and they forget that it points us toward God. The problem is technically called "bibliolatry," which means making an idol out of the Bible. This occurs in some circles that emphasize doctrine or Bible study to the point of neglecting a personal relationship with Jesus, who said that the Scriptures actually bear witness to him (John 5:39).
>
> A preacher once said this is like the man who goes to a restaurant and reads the menu. Then, exclaiming how great the menu is, he puts salt and pepper on it and proceeds to eat it.[2]

Reading the Bible to gain information-focused knowledge for the purpose of elevating one's standing or advantage over others will neither nourish the reader nor lead others to faith. For example, it is tempting to read the Bible and assume that it is good and right to pray for vengeance because people in scriptural stories do. The Old Testament records several prayers that go far beyond asking for protection *against* an enemy (Psalms 44, 70, 74; Jeremiah 18:23). They are malicious, asking for the *destruction* of the enemy. When godly Nehemiah was ridiculed and threatened by Sanballat and Tobiah, he prayed passionately for the destruction of his critics: "Hear us, O our God, for we are despised. Turn their insults back on their own heads. Give them over as plunder in a land of captivity. Do not cover up their guilt or blot out their sins from your sight, for they have thrown insults in the face of the builders" (Nehemiah 4:4-5).

But Jesus and the teachers of the New Testament took exception to the imprecatory prayers of the Old Testament. The powerful grace and love of Jesus Christ confronted all vengeful mentalities and threw them down forever when he said: "You have heard that it was said, 'Love your neighbor and hate your enemy.' But I tell you, love your enemies and pray for those who persecute you, that you may be children of your Father in heaven" (Matthew 5:43-45 TNIV). Echoing Jesus' directive, the Apostle Paul wrote to the church in Rome: "Bless those who persecute you; bless and do not curse" (Romans 12:14). Jesus had reframed the entire conversation.

The church today must listen to Jesus' voice in order to interpret the Bible correctly. We can assume that if Jesus and Paul were commanding people to love and bless their enemies, we should also extend love to everybody on the continuum—irritating people; disagreeable people; people of various political bents; those who look at life differently; individuals who appreciate different music. The list goes on and on. As people in God's church we must ruthlessly push back the natural bent to love people like us and hate the people we disagree with. Without exception, as Christ followers, we are called to love and bless, showing grace and patience to everyone. Any response less than this is not Christlike and is wrong.

In an age where the Christian church is perceived by some in America to be as angry and intolerant as its critics, Christians of this century would do well to read, reflect, and respond like Jesus when critics lob destructive threats and insults. The lavish grace and love of God in Jesus Christ is so strong that we, like Jesus, should have no need for vengeance or name-calling. If we are settled, mature, and deeply rooted in our personal relationship and understanding of God, the sheer presence of God in our lives draws us away from fear and defensiveness. If God is who he says he is, and Jesus is powerfully present through the Holy Spirit, we will have a deep and abiding confidence in the face of even the worst of critics. Indeed, we even have the capacity to pour out compassion on those we individually view as our critics and enemies and pray for their well-being.

The Bible as a Spiritual Discipline

Anyone can read the Bible as a reference book to learn biblical facts or behavioral guidelines, but it is the daily spiritual discipline of Bible reading and meditation on God's word that entices believers to encounter God and to be changed. The Bible is given to us for spiritual formation and nourishment, yet some Christians have never learned that reading and meditating on Scripture can be transformative.

Jesus' disciple-turned-apostle Paul wrote to the new church in Rome that all people can see proof of God through **general revelation** in God's creation. "Since the creation of the world God's invisible qualities—his eternal power and divine nature—have been clearly seen, being understood from what has been made, so that people are without excuse" (Romans 1:20 TNIV). God sending his word in the form of Jesus to all of humanity (John 1:1) is a **special revelation**. He also spoke his word through personal address into the lives of people (Deuteronomy 18:18-20; Jeremiah 1:9; and 1 Samuel 15:3). But it was through the power of God in the *written* books of the Bible that he gave the most direct special revelation. By knowing the Bible, we begin to know God and how to live today.

The church must encourage this ancient spiritual discipline of deeply experiencing and absorbing the life-altering word of God. People—young people in particular—will be intrigued to learn that the Christian faith offers this sort of supernatural power. It is

a truth that has not been widely promoted. Spiritual transformation is a mystery and a gift, and the time is ripe. Young new
believers are demonstrating their openness to and interest in
ancient practices of faith in their styles of worship, incorporating
everything from ancient poetry, classical art, and candles to alternative rock music.

> Blessed are those
>> who do not walk in step with the wicked
>> or stand in the way that sinners take
>> or sit in the company of mockers,
> but who delight in the law of the LORD
>> and meditate on his law day and night. (Psalm 1:1-2 TNIV)

The psalmist uses a beautiful metaphor from nature to describe
what happens when people practice this discipline:

> They are like a tree planted by streams of water,
>> which yields its fruit in season
>> and whose leaf does not wither—
> whatever they do prospers. (Psalm 1:3 TNIV)

Scripture nourishes us like water nourishes a sapling tree,
enabling it to grow strong. Taking in the wisdom of God is the
first step in growing people who will then participate in a vibrant,
missional church.

The Bible is God's holy revelation to humans. God's purpose
for revelation is to draw people closer to him, not primarily to
keep them in line. People do not often encounter God through
thunderbolts, but often do through sacred text. His desire for relationship is signified by his revealed message to the church.

Living Out Scripture

The word of God, illuminated by the power of the Holy Spirit, is not passive. "Your word is a lamp to my feet and a light for my path," says Psalm 119:105. The Bible actively leads us along our journey. It is a practical and positive guide to our behavior and choices. We are bombarded by advertising messages, Internet news, blogs, e-mails, texts, and calls. The Bible can seem like just another set of words unless we help people make Scripture real and applicable. Consider the difference when we actually put the Bible into practice. Imagine a woman reading the words of Philippians 4:8 (TNIV): "Finally, brothers and sisters, whatever is true, whatever is noble, whatever is right, whatever is pure, whatever is lovely, whatever is admirable—if anything is excellent or praiseworthy—think about such things." What do these words mean to her? Imagine her deciding to spend time actually doing what the verses command to see if something more than her obedience will result. Imagine her amazement at a metamorphosis that could only be described as mystical—God changing her actions and thoughts and words through the act of her resolution. It is just a beginning, but an encouraging one. Obedience enables her to experience God more closely.

If the church is serious about sharing the beauty of life in God's presence, the Christians it nurtures must be living out their faith in tangible ways.

The ancient people of faith in the Old Testament had a holistic view of Scripture. God's word was not to be dispassionately read and then set aside. The Torah (literally, "Law") was central not just in worship. The people understood that it was to be infused into every aspect of life and into the entire community of faith.

The same is true for us now. Church leaders are called to help believers infuse the Bible into every part of human life. It should be in our thoughts and in our actions. It can be part of the words we speak to strangers, the attitude we have toward people of different backgrounds, and the way we spend our leisure time. It can be part of the e-mail text, the prayer, and the worship service. Every time Christians pick up the Bible or recall a verse or apply a scriptural principle they should view it as an opportunity to take a drink of God and live out his word. The church provides ample opportunities for Christians and non-Christians to investigate Scripture, wrestle with God's word, and apply it to life.

True Story

Carie's relationship with Bible reading was not always a loving one. Secretly, she viewed Bible reading as a chore with very little reward. The day-by-day Bible guides helped a bit, but the Gospels were by now too familiar to be fascinating and the Old Testament genealogies, war stories, and Hebrew laws were tedious at best, and sometimes bizarre and off-putting.

At the encouragement of a Christian mentor, Carie decided to stop reading only for morals she could apply to her own life. She stopped pressuring the Bible to release its secrets all at once. Instead, Carie tried *experiencing* Scripture for transformation. She began praying before reading. She read thoughtfully but without insisting that she immediately understand all that she read. She spent time deciphering what she read, considering the context of the writings, and noting how God communicated with the

---

Israelites, how Jesus responded to detractors, and what Paul wrote to the early members of the Christian church. Carie saw herself in the stories of deeply flawed individuals trying to live by faith, and felt comfort. She read by candlelight, outdoors, with music, and out loud.

Through the Bible she heard God's voice—sometimes in a whisper, sometimes clearly through repetition and pattern. Carie began to *experience* God through the words of Scripture.

Learning from Lives

People long to be immersed in stories. The story form has expanded over time, from spoken to written to drama to film, but people are still drawn to tales of human conflict, sacrifice, and redemption. From *Beowulf* to *MacBeth* to *Jane Eyre* to *To Kill a Mockingbird* to *A Raisin in the Sun*, great literature speaks to us. In 2007, Americans bought nearly 1.4 billion tickets to see movies.[3] Hollywood screenwriting lecturer Robert McKee said, "The story arts have become humanity's prime source of inspiration, as it seeks to order chaos and gain insight into life."[4]

The word of God offers the church stories of personal transformation and triumph. Often these stories are tales of an ordinary protagonist, a person caught up in the trials and crises of life, and they can be beautifully relevant in a contemporary context.

A man working against policies that overtly discriminate against African Americans reads the story of Moses standing up against Pharaoh. In God's command "Let my people go" he recognizes the power of the supernatural against what looks to be impossible-to-defeat oppression.

A hardworking business executive finds herself completely overlooked for development and promotion. God sits with her as she reads the biblical leadership stories of Joseph and David. She sees again how God honors faithfulness and accomplishes his will in unexpected ways.

A frightened, heartsick widow reads that God is "a father to the fatherless, a defender of widows . . . [and] sets the lonely in families" (Psalm 68:5-6). She recognizes God's intervention when a long-lost acquaintance contacts her and reestablishes a friendship.

A young man trapped in addiction reads about the Apostle Paul, who suffered with an unnamed "thorn" in the flesh. Paul wrote:

> Three times I pleaded with the Lord to take it away from me. But he said to me, "My grace is sufficient for you, for my power is made perfect in weakness." Therefore I will boast all the more gladly about my weaknesses, so that Christ's power may rest on me. That is why, for Christ's sake, I delight in weaknesses, in insults, in hardships, in persecutions, in difficulties. For when I am weak, then I am strong. (2 Corinthians 12:8-10)

Though doubtful of his own ability to resist old temptations, the young man begins again to seek an exit from addiction and to move toward hope through an encompassing relationship with Jesus.

A teenage girl, completely worn out from running away—from God, family, and problems that follow her everywhere—reads the words: "Come to me, all you who are weary and burdened, and I will give you rest. Take my yoke upon you and learn from me, for I am gentle and humble in heart, and you will find rest for your souls. For my yoke is easy and my burden is light" (Matthew 11:28-30). She prays for God's help to find escape and a way home.

The church must show the timelessness of the Bible through old stories of hope.

God's Word—Alive

Sometimes we read the Bible and we are cut to the heart. God's word shines on our path, but it also shines on our souls, seeking to change us and right our relationship with God.

> For the word of God is living and active. Sharper than any double-edged sword, it penetrates even to dividing soul and spirit, joints and marrow; it judges the thoughts and attitudes of the heart. Nothing in all creation is hidden from God's sight. Everything is uncovered and laid bare before the eyes of him to whom we must give account. (Hebrews 4:12-13)

Bob experienced God's living word unexpectedly one Sunday during a worship service. A short drama captured the brief vignette of a man who unwillingly comes home after the death of his grandfather to make peace with family members. Watching the drama, Bob felt the vague pang of recognition. The words of Romans 12:18 came to his mind: "If it is possible, as far as it depends on you, live at peace with everyone" (Romans 12:18). Although he had long justified the antagonistic relationship with his sister through years of pain and dysfunction, he now felt called to be with her and try to make amends. He purchased an expensive overseas ticket and prepared himself spiritually for the painful and—he prayed—healing encounter.

The living word of God cuts, but it also heals.

Judy was someone people described as "godly." She was devout in her prayer life and clear minded and focused in her spiritual discipline of Bible reading. She was invited to pray for a man dying of cancer. After several days without a good night's sleep, the man was weary, discouraged, and miserable. Judy met with him and prayed selections from Psalm 4:

> Answer me when I call to you,
>   O my righteous God.
> Give me relief from my distress;
>   be merciful to me and hear my prayer. . . .
> I will lie down and sleep in peace,
>   for you alone, O LORD,
> make me dwell in safety. (vv. 1, 8)

A sudden and gentle peace overcame him while she read that psalm in a prayerlike fashion. Shortly thereafter the man fell asleep and had his first full night's rest in several days.

God's word is living and active, serving very real purposes in our lives today.

Applying the Word of God with Humility

Some people are uninterested in God and the Bible because they have encountered Christians who were reckless with their interpretation of Scripture. Misinterpretations of God's word have led some to believe that Christianity is an angry, bigoted, and judgmental faith. Defensiveness can give the impression that some Christians are more concerned about defending their view of the Bible than living out what's in it.

Christians must admit that the larger perception of Jesus ought to be one of grace, humility, forgiveness, healing, and redemption. When we live God's word rather than hammering others with it we live out 2 Timothy 2:15; we do our best to present ourselves to God as ones who do not need to be ashamed, but who correctly handle the word of truth.

This is the humble and dynamic approach to God's word.

> Do nothing out of selfish ambition or vain conceit, but in humility consider others better than yourselves. Each of you should look not only to your own interests, but also to the interests of others.
> Your attitude should be the same as that of Christ Jesus:
> Who, being in very nature God,
>   did not consider equality with God
>   something to be grasped,
> but made himself nothing,
>   taking the very nature of a servant. (Philippians 2:3-7)

Biblically inspired Christians *experience* God's word and live it. They do not own it. They do not brandish it. Only then can the word of God transform them into humble servants. It can join Christians together in loving and effective communities of faith. Religion locks people out; the Bible invites them in. The church holds the keys to this new outlook.

Discovering Timeless Texts

The Bible is not a static document; it is dynamic, lively, meaningful, and mystically timely not only to individual daily life but to the life of the church. As the prophet Isaiah said, "The grass withers and the flowers fall, but the word of our God stands forever" (Isaiah 40:8).

Living out a transformative missional faith in today's culture begins with God's sacred text. That is not new. But the church today must have a right understanding of how to read it, understand it, and share it with others. Through thoughtful, humble, and active application of biblical truth the church will offer an irresistible and transformative treasure to a new, intrigued audience.

Heavenly Father, teach your twenty-first-century church to drink your word like a tree rooted along a river. Help us form spiritual disciplines that lead us on paths to experience you. Give us the big picture of your plan and show us, even in small ways, how you desire us to fit into it. Holy Spirit of God, illuminate the path in front of us and every corner of our souls. Jesus, our living revelation of God, teach us the way of gentleness and servanthood as we handle your truth with respect, living it out with grace and integrity. We pray this in Jesus' name. Amen.

Start Translating

1. Guide your congregation through these personal reflection questions:

   Where, how, and when do you read the Bible? Do you feel at peace or hurried? Ask God to give you a tranquil heart.

   What obstacles in your life keep you from reading and studying the Bible? How can you change them?

   What are your motivations for reading the Bible? If you want to change those motivations, write a note to remind yourself to pray for a change.

2. Honestly look at ways that people in your church community have used the Bible inappropriately. List at least two ways that improper practices can be eliminated from the church DNA.

3. As a church, how can you become more aware of your broader culture's perception of the Bible? What barriers do people in your community and culture have to the Bible? How can your congregation demonstrate a more Christlike understanding of the purpose of Scripture?

4. Discuss the level of engagement your congregation has in the Bible. Are people talking about their study of the Bible in ordinary conversation? Do people share stories of how the Bible has encouraged them and how they are encouraging others?

5. Consider printed or online tools that can be shared with your congregation to increase its experience of the Bible as a tool for personal spiritual growth.

6. Differentiate between major doctrines, minor doctrines, and subjective opinion. Ask hard questions: "Are we focusing on particular passages instead of the whole body of biblical instruction?"

7. Is your congregation literate in the various genres of biblical literature? Is it sensitive to the priority of not using verses out of context? If the answer to these questions is no, list ways that you can immediately begin to educate your community on the cultural and historical contexts of Scripture through special training, guest speakers, or classes.

CHAPTER TWO

PRAYER DESIGNED

Relying on the Supernatural

The LORD is near to all who call on him,
to all who call on him in truth.
He fulfills the desires of those who fear him;
he hears their cry and saves them. (Psalm 145:18-19)

The church cannot live without prayer. Most Christians would agree with this basic tenet, and there is some evidence that we believe it. In worship we participate in corporate prayer. Believers facing illness or difficulty share prayer requests and receive heartfelt promises of "I will pray for you." We pray before meals and with our children at bedtime.

But as the church stirs restlessly in a new time and context, we look out at a disorienting landscape and wonder if we are praying well. We see a culture that is spiritually charged but aloof to Christian faith—doing fine without it, in fact (at least on the surface of things)—and sometimes deeply antagonistic to it. Churches are in decline. Some are fading away; others are dying. Because we believe deeply in living out and expanding the hopeful message of

Jesus, we are confused and embarrassed by the disinterest and disdain of people around us. In the face of their rejection, some people of faith call on God to bring a revival. They decry sin and call for restoration in very broad terms. But in that approach we are failing to recognize that God has first called *us* to be restored.

In the Old Testament as King Solomon was initiating his leadership, he had a conversation with God, who reminded him that there might come a time when it all would go wrong. If that happened, Solomon was instructed to pray. God said,

> If my people, who are called by my name, will humble themselves and pray and seek my face and turn from their wicked ways, then will I hear from heaven and will forgive their sin and will heal their land. Now my eyes will be open and my ears attentive to the prayers offered in this place. (2 Chronicles 7:14-15)

Only by being humbled, by recognizing our own failure to lean on God, can we hope to regain God's perspective, power, and provision for our lives and ministries. Prayer is the starting point of the journey of humility as we seek to reorient ourselves with God's plans and provision.

What has gone wrong? What failures do we need to confess? What are our "wicked ways" for which we must humbly ask forgiveness? Principally, the power of God's lavish grace and holistic beauty of life in Jesus Christ has failed to be lived out by Christians and furthermore translated into twenty-first-century terms. God's message is no less attractive, eloquent, or life changing, but the people to whom we bring the message have changed, and the church has not paid attention to the rapidly accelerating transformations in culture. Insulated, afraid, entrenched, and defensive, we have blamed society, refused to engage with certain kinds of individuals, and then asked God why our churches are not introducing new people to faith. Our sensibilities should be stunned by the knowledge that 80 percent of Americans do not attend a church of any kind.[1]

In our self-reflection it is painful to see how little we have *relied* on the role of prayer for our translation work. Prayer is slotted and scheduled, but it is sometimes—if we are frank—a tier-two activity, part of the activity of worship but not the essence of our relationship with God. An utter dependence on prayer has dwindled almost to extinction. We do it, but with prayer as a side dish, something to be tasted during the service, not the lifeblood of our faith.

Recognizing the Need

How did we arrive here? In the decades when resources were ample and church attendance assured, prayer became secondary to organizing, strategizing, designing service styles, and implementing programs—that is, *doing church*. We grew confident in our ability to attract people, all while the practice of prayer receded. We might agree that prayer is life-sustaining to the church, but we do not practice it as if it truly were, depending on it to guide us to new ways of practicing our faith. The church cannot pragmatically plan itself into the future.

The timing of this introspection is good. Some people who are exhausted by a world that offers little hope are hungry for something *more*. Christians have an opportunity to offer care, a giving and forgiving faith, and the immense peace of a relationship with God. We can offer simplicity for those wounded by a burdensome or legalistic tradition. We can offer bottomless complexity for those seeking intellectual and spiritual insight.

As reality forces a recalibration, the church, too, is ready. We are asking ourselves uncomfortable questions. "Are we giving the proper emphasis and credit to prayer?" "Should we be doing it a different way or just *more*?" It is no longer enough to expand programs, send direct mail, and run Christmas Eve and Easter service ads. These are good things that help us communicate with people around us. But communicating with God is the only way the church will tap into the supernatural and invite genuine change.

Where Do We Start?

Our model is Jesus. In his relationship with his twelve disciples, Jesus taught the centrality of prayer. He served them as a mentor and role model. He taught them how to pray. He spent time praying *with* them and *for* them. He separated himself and prayed alone; he must have expected them to do the same. And he used an organic image of vine and branches to describe the power they had in prayer.

> I am the vine; you are the branches. If you remain in me and I in you, you will bear much fruit; apart from me you can do nothing. If you do not remain in me, you are like a branch that is thrown away and withers; such branches are picked up, thrown into the fire and burned. If you remain in me and my words remain in you, ask whatever you wish, and it will be done for you. This is to my Father's glory, that you bear much fruit, showing yourselves to be my disciples. (John 15:5-8 TNIV)

Jesus' metaphor shows that vines and branches are in living relationship with each other. The church is a branch that continually draws its nourishment, power, and life from Jesus, the vine. When Jesus said, "Apart from me you can do nothing," he made it clear that when we do not pray or commune with him we are functionally ripping ourselves off the vine and starving our faith—and the church—to death. James, an early church leader, wrote: "Come near to God and he will come near to you" (James 4:8). It is an exhortation and a compelling promise.

This understanding of prayer is the same for the church. Prayer is the means by which churches, leaders, and Christians connect with the power and current activity of God in their time and place. If we start with prayer—and continue to pray fervently—all of the other important leadership disciplines (e.g., reading books, making strategic plans, going to conferences, and so on) are better positioned to be infused with God's voice and perspective. The needed reorientation is to move away from a strictly ingrained pragmatic methodology and embrace the mysterious practice of prayer in which God will give us Holy Spirit–guided discernment and direction.

Moving Forward, Step by Step

Leaders of prayer groups complain that it is hard to get people out to "just" pray. Active Christians are willing to handle many of the functions of church but may be less inclined to devote precious time to confess, adore, thank, and listen. If we look this deficit in the eye and see only an opportunity to begin Wednesday night prayer meetings, we have missed the point and we will run headlong into failure. Let's admit it. Weekly prayer meetings often devolve into too few people praying too few things with too little power. Corporate prayer needs to be more fluid and dynamic and less predictable or scheduled. God is calling us to prayer, not programs.

How, then, do we enact this dramatic process of change?

1. Recognize and confess that we have not believed in prayer. We have marketed, created niches, thrown in some prayers, and tossed the mixture like a salad. We need to saturate the church in prayer.

2. Awaken to the realization that prayer has preceded every significant movement of people to faith, notably the three great spiritual awakenings in American history—the 1730s, early 1800s, and the late nineteenth and early twentieth centuries. In each instance the church stopped blaming culture, government, or secularism and took a long hard look at itself. The believers in those times had Nehemiah moments of confession of sin and returning to the promises of God. Like Nehemiah, Christians experienced God's closeness, answer to prayer, and a new day of restoration.

3. Rather than developing a plan to obligate or compel Christians to pray, ask God to call your community to prayer. Jesus said, "I will do whatever you ask in my name, so that the Son may bring glory to the Father. You may ask me for anything in my name, and I will do it" (John 14:13-14). God moves; we follow. Rather than prescribing our desires, we listen to God's, asking him only to lead us where he is working in this world.

4. Make yourselves available to do as God directs. Ministry works best when we have heard from God and are doing what he wants us to do. Psalm 127:1 reminds us:

> Unless the LORD builds the house,
>   its builders labor in vain.
> Unless the LORD watches over the city,
>   the watchmen stand guard in vain.

We stop trusting in tips, hints, practices, and grids, and seek his movement in the world first.

5. Trust that God *will* lead his church.

6. Persevere. In order to experience the spirit of God we need an open sense of prayer without time lines. We pray, wait, and work as God leads us. Imagine God speaking to us throughout the day as frequently as our friends send us text messages. It is normal behavior to read and quickly respond to dozens of messages that come to our phones. Imagine what our prayer lives would be like if we were open to receiving and sending that sort of spontaneous and constant communication between God and us in a continual dialogue throughout our days.

Prayer is how believers actively follow the biblical command "Love the Lord your God." Love is about relationship, and a rich relationship with God is fully centered on prayer, both individually and in our faith communities. God desires closeness with his people. We cannot pray and hold him at arm's length.

For the Christian *and* the church, prayer is *the* primary method of growth. We do not always think of prayer in this light. Christians may more likely pray as a method of showing respect, fulfilling an obligation, or having wishes granted. Learning about prayer and practicing it more deliberately opens us to a deeper faith experience.

Approaching without Reservations

Sometimes there are barriers to the prayer life of the church. If we have not learned the discipline of taking time, we pray infrequently—or not at all.

We can be intimidated by praying, doubting our ability to pray well. We do not have the gift. We do not have the words. Deep down we may believe we do not have the right. Some of us hear other people doing it eloquently and gracefully, which makes us feel inadequate and self-conscious. In his book *Prayer: Finding the Heart's True Home*, Richard Foster notes:

> We believe prayer is something we should do, even something we want to do, but it seems like a chasm stands between us and actually praying. . . . It is the notion—almost universal among us modern high achievers—that we have to have everything "just right" in order to pray. That is, before we can really pray, our lives need some fine-tuning, or we need to know more about how to pray, or we need to study the philosophical questions surrounding prayer, or we need to have a better grasp of the great traditions of prayer.[2]

But Jesus put concerns to rest when he taught about prayer and relationship with God through his favorite lesson form, the parable. The New Testament biographer Luke captured Jesus' short story of the Pharisee and the tax collector.

> To some who were confident of their own righteousness and looked down on everyone else, Jesus told this parable: "Two men went up to the temple to pray, one a Pharisee and the other a tax collector. The Pharisee stood by himself and prayed: 'God, I thank you that I am not like other people—robbers, evildoers, adulterers—or even like this tax collector. I fast twice a week and give a tenth of all I get.'
>
> "But the tax collector stood at a distance. He would not even look up to heaven, but beat his breast and said, 'God, have mercy on me, a sinner.'
>
> "I tell you that this man, rather than the other, went home justified before God. For all those who exalt themselves will be

humbled, and those who humble themselves will be exalted."
(Luke 18:9-14 TNIV)

Every parable had a moral. This one taught that it was not high position, technique, experience praying in front of a crowd, or confidence that enabled a connection with God. The tax collector called out to God, broken down and humbled. He came in genuine fear of the Lord. Fear in this context does not mean being afraid of God. Rather, it is the acknowledgement that God is God: all-powerful and worthy of respect, honor, and obedience. In that state of recognition, the tax collector was ready to be heard by God and to hear from him. The story suggests a door opening, the beginning of a relationship. Having approached God once, the tax collector would return to God's comforting presence for ongoing forgiveness and peace.

Christians may grow discouraged about their prayer lives when they do not *feel* any immediate presence of God, blaming themselves for not being spiritual enough, or beginning to doubt the reality of God's presence. The regular discipline of prayer is the answer to this sense of dryness and disconnection. God designed people to communicate with him, and prayer is the supernatural method he created. We must push through the boredom and barriers, trusting that he intended for us to experience the spiritual rewards of prayer.

Jesus specifically taught that sincere, repentant people who come to God enter God's presence. The tax collector in the story represented the most hated and immoral person of his time. If *he* could approach God, we can be sure God welcomes our prayers, too, and invites us in.

A Varied Prayer Life

Many people in the church today long for a rich prayer life, but even those who have prayed all their lives may resort to familiar, rote prayers ("Bless this food to our bodies"; "Be with us"), self-serving prayers ("Give us a good day"), or self-righteous prayers ("God, convict those who . . ."). But there is endless variety in prayer, as the Bible outlines in rich detail and examples. The church can rediscover the variety available in prayer.

The Prayer of Communion

Some prayers are purely meant to seek God's presence, just to be with him. These communications are not the making of lists or the asking of questions. They are simply times of being with God. Psalm 61:1-5 (TNIV) is a beautiful example of a prayer of communion with God:

Hear my cry, O God;
  listen to my prayer.
From the ends of the earth I call to you,
  I call as my heart grows faint;
lead me to the rock that is higher than I.
  For you have been my refuge,
a strong tower against the foe.
  I long to dwell in your tent forever
and take refuge in the shelter of your wings.
  For you, God, have heard my vows;
you have given me the heritage of those who fear your name.

This is a love letter and an acknowledgment of God's central position in our lives.

The Prayer of Intercession

The New Testament teacher James wrote: "Pray for each other so that you may be healed. The prayer of a righteous person is powerful and effective" (James 5:16 TNIV). God invites Christians to partner with him to meet the needs of other people. He asks his followers to pray for friends, acquaintances, neighbors, enemies, and strangers. When we intercede on their behalf we are seeking their good—tangibly serving and loving them. We may not learn the outcome of our prayers for some time—or ever—but we have the assurance that we are doing what God asks us to do.

True Story

Lily discovered a ministry to others when she started bringing her therapy dog to provide encouragement to people in isolation. In her volunteer work, she was assigned an assisted living facility one week, a children's hospital another. One day she visited with young men at a juvenile detention center. At first they appeared flippant, but they were drawn to the stunts of the little dog. As the dog went from boy to boy in search of attention, one of the teens asked, "So, is your dog a good luck charm?"

Odd question. "Why do you ask?" Lily asked.

"I just found out I could go on trial as an adult. I need all the luck I can get."

She could hear the fear in his voice. Her heart went out to him as she suddenly saw the boy behind the brash posturing. Lily answered, "My dog doesn't bring good luck, but I'll pray for you. Prayer is better than luck."

The boy stood abruptly and walked away, but he returned several minutes later. "Did you mean that?" he asked. "You'll pray for me?"

"Yes," she said. "We can pray together right now."

Before she could begin, another boy asked, "Can you pray for me too?" And then a third added, "I need prayer. What about me?" They were still acting tough but there seemed to be a real desire for the prayer beneath the posturing.

Lily read a few Bible passages about God's concern for their future. Then she prayed on their behalf for God's mercy in their time of urgent need.

For weeks Lily continued to pray for the boys at the center. She felt nourished by the prayer and closer to the young men she had befriended. They sought her out each time she arrived at the detention center. Maybe they felt nourished, too.

The Prayer of Petition

The New Testament author John wrote: "This is the confidence we have in approaching God: that if we ask anything according to his will, he hears us. And if we know that he hears us—whatever we ask—we know that we have what we asked of him" (1 John 5:14-15). This is a potent claim. Can the church recognize that John's teaching is true while acknowledging that God is not our own personal Santa Claus or a genie in a lamp? John says, "If we ask anything according to his will, he hears us." How do we know the will of God? It is not always easy or quick.

The church continues the search and discovery. Often we can

discern God's will through the basic truths of the Bible. We know it is his will that we forgive others, so we should pray for the ability to forgive. It is God's will that we acknowledge God as the provider of our everyday needs. It is God's will that we are generous with others and care for people needing help. But, there are other life situations that are more difficult to discern. How do we choose between two courses of action when neither is pleasant or ideal? How do we deal with a difficult person? How do we cope with loss, illness, and disappointment? These decisions require multiple conversations with God. There will be gray areas. It is a process. Patience will be necessary.

The Prayer of Submission

The most poignant example of a prayer of submission comes from Jesus right before his arrest and crucifixion. He knew the intense trouble that was boiling up among religious leaders in Jerusalem. He was aware that his friend Judas was about to betray him. Jesus understood his purpose. The convergence of these realities created a horrifying future. He took his disciples to a place called Gethsemane and asked them to wait for him while he prayed.

> Going a little farther, he fell with his face to the ground and prayed, "My Father, if it is possible, may this cup be taken from me. Yet not as I will, but as you will."
> Then he returned to his disciples and found them sleeping. "Couldn't you men keep watch with me for one hour?" he asked Peter. "Watch and pray so that you will not fall into temptation. The spirit is willing, but the flesh is weak."
> He went away a second time and prayed, "My Father, if it is not possible for this cup to be taken away unless I drink it, may your will be done."

When he came back, he again found them sleeping, because their eyes were heavy. So he left them and went away once more and prayed the third time, saying the same thing. (Matthew 26:39-44 TNIV)

Jesus struggled, knowing what was ahead, and prayed three times, each time submitting to what he knew was God's plan: "Not as I will, but as you will." When he did not experience a complete lifting of his distress and anguish, he returned to God, asking again. In the end, however, he submitted completely—spiritually, emotionally, and physically. Prayer was the avenue to this submission. It is ours, too.

The Prayer of Confession

David was a Bible "great," a man whose love for God seems epic. His writings are passionate and expressive. But he was also deeply flawed. We read about his repeated errors in judgment, his cruelty, his selfishness, and his blatant immoral behavior. It is not surprising that some of the psalms he wrote are devoted to contrition.

Then I acknowledged my sin to you
    and did not cover up my iniquity.
I said, "I will confess my transgressions to the LORD."
    And you forgave the guilt of my sin.
Therefore let all the faithful pray to you
    while you may be found;
surely the rising of the mighty waters will not reach them.
    You are my hiding place;
you will protect me from trouble
    and surround me with songs of deliverance.
                              (Psalm 32:5-7 TNIV)

David's prayers show how a close, one-on-one relationship with God can be obstructed by sin and then restored through confession. This is a lesson for Christians *and* the church.

Another Old Testament hero, Daniel, demonstrated a prayer of confession that covered a multitude of people—all of Israel. "I prayed to the LORD my God and confessed. . . . We have sinned and done wrong. We have been wicked and have rebelled; we have turned away from your commands and laws. We have not listened" (Daniel 9:4-6). After his heartfelt confession he concluded with a request:

> Now, our God, hear the prayers and petitions of your servant. For your sake, Lord, look with favor on your desolate sanctuary. Give ear, our God, and hear; open your eyes and see the desolation of the city that bears your Name. We do not make requests of you because we are righteous, but because of your great mercy. Lord, listen! Lord, forgive! Lord, hear and act! For your sake, my God, do not delay, because your city and your people bear your Name. (Daniel 9:17-19 TNIV)

There is an acknowledgment of God's goodness and an urgent call for help. We must pray for the church and the people in it.

The Prayer of Thanksgiving

David wrote: "Give thanks to the LORD, for he is good; his love endures forever" (Psalm 106:1). This verse suggests that it is appropriate to thank God because of what he is—righteous, holy, and good.

It is also right to thank God for specific blessings. The practice of real thankfulness is a vital spiritual practice, one that can be neglected among American Christians. We are accustomed to the provision of not only food, shelter, clothing, and clean water to sustain life, but also an *abundance* of goods—furniture, vehicles, recreational equipment, electronics, kitchen utensils, appliances, and more. We are no longer surprised by our access to high quality restaurants, gourmet groceries, vacations, costly memberships, and retirements; we view them as well earned. In this age of reward and gratification, an attitude of thankfulness and reflection is a discipline that will contribute depth to our prayer lives. Constant thanksgiving shows a recognition of how much we have while others have little. It can prompt us to a different view of blessings and change the way we live in a desperate world.

The Prayer of Complaint

A prayer of complaint is not grumbling. It is deeper and more serious. Prayers of complaint exist in several places in the Bible, particularly in the Old Testament book of Psalms. David, whom God promised would become a king, had not seen that promise come to pass and was forced to live as a nomadic refugee in a damp cave.

> I cry aloud to the LORD;
>> I lift up my voice to the LORD for mercy.
> I pour out my complaint before him;
>> before him I tell my trouble.
> When my spirit grows faint within me,
>> it is you who know my way.
> In the path where I walk
>> men have hidden a snare for me.
> Look to my right and see;
>> no one is concerned for me.

I have no refuge;
no one cares for my life. (Psalm 142:1-4)

Imagine this as a modern prayer, spoken by members of a church who have been passionate in their pursuit of revival for their church. The congregation is made up of godly people who have dedicated themselves to nurturing God's church. Their future has not turned out as they imagined. They have an unfulfilled dream—the dream of seeing their community of faith come alive again so it can bless the people of the city. Where is God? Does he care? The people are just in their complaint. They could easily pray something like David's prayer.

> I cry to you, O LORD;
> I say, "You are my refuge,
> my portion in the land of the living."
> Listen to my cry,
> for I am in desperate need;
> rescue me from those who pursue me,
> for they are too strong for me.
> Set me free from my prison. (Psalm 142:5-7)

There is a difficult tension here. Prayers of complaint to God include the dimension of persistence and fervency, but they must also, at some critical point, transform into submission. Theologian D. G. Bloesch summed this up when he wrote:

> Biblical prayer includes . . . both wrestling with God in the darkness and resting in the stillness. There is a time to argue and complain to God, but there is also a time to submit. . . . Prayer is both pleading with God that he will hear and act upon our requests and a trusting surrender to God in the confidence that he will act in his own time and way. But the confidence comes only through the struggle.[3]

Knowing How to Pray

How do we know the "correct" way to pray? Jesus' disciples wanted to know, too. In Matthew 6, Jesus gave specific directions. His words contain important information for all who pray.

1. Do not be hypocritical. If we pray to be noticed, we are not being honest and we are not focusing on God.
2. Pray unpretentiously—that is, without needing to be noticed—to God, the Father, who is "unseen."
3. We do not need a lot of words to impress or convince God. He knows what we want before we ask.

Jesus shared a prayer that covered the vital aspects of communication with God.

> Our Father in heaven,
> hallowed be your name,
> your kingdom come,
> your will be done,
> on earth as it is in heaven.
> Give us today our daily bread.
> And forgive us our debts,
> as we also have forgiven our debtors.
> And lead us not into temptation,
> but deliver us from the evil one.
> For if you forgive others when they sin against you, your heavenly Father will also forgive you. But if you do not forgive others their sins, your Father will not forgive your sins.
>
> (Matthew 6:9b-15 TNIV)

We pray in faith. We pray not just for our own needs and desires, but also for God's kingdom, in heaven *and* on earth. We request forgiveness, realizing that we must not harbor grudges against others.

The posture of our prayer is up to us. Variations are demonstrated in the Bible—raising arms, bowing down, kneeling, sitting, standing, and even sometimes praying completely prostrate, face-down on the ground before God. Depending on the circumstances, we may fold our hands, clench our fists, hold them open and upright, or cover our heads. We may walk or rock. Our eyes can be open or closed. Prayer is not a "one size fits all" practice. Our prayers can be spoken, sung, drawn, danced, or written. Being created unique we have our own preferences that contribute to our experience of prayer.

The church can help worshipers practice new forms of prayer within the worship service—and outside of it. Each week include a new exercise in prayer. Try silent prayer, allowing enough time for participants to focus on a particular directive. Incorporate a responsive prayer backed by music. Invite worshipers to read written prayers. Speak the words of a hymn as a prayer. Write prayers, create a small photocopied packet, and ask community members to take them home to pray in solitude. (Imagine the power of knowing that all the people in the church are praying the same prayers, together, during the week.) By inviting individuals to break out of their routines, you will invite variation and freshness into the life of the church.

Making Prayer Central

Prayer is the spiritual oxygen of the Christian community. We cannot live without it. Jesus spoke several times about prayer and its value in church life. Mark 11:15-17 records a telling story. In Jerusalem, crooked business people were taking advantage of vulnerable guest worshipers in the temple area, out-of-towners who needed money exchanged so they could buy the animals required for the annual temple worship. These pilgrims were being cheated. Jesus saw this and was furious. He rushed the temple courts and pushed over tables, shouting at the merchants. The Gospel accounts describe him "driving out those who were buying and selling there." It was holy anger. "Is it not written: 'My house will be a house of prayer for all nations'? But you have made it 'a den of robbers'" (TNIV).

Jesus could have defined the temple of God in many terms. He could have said, "My house will be a house of worship, great teaching, beautiful architecture, and really nice people." He did not. Quoting the Old Testament prophet Isaiah, he said, "My house will be a house of prayer for all nations."

There is a general understanding that prayer should be part of the individual Christian's life. We need to have that same expectation of the church. How often do we pray together? Many churches have social groups, music groups, support groups, youth groups, and even sports teams. These are all good things, but if prayer is not interwoven we will never attain all that God has in mind for his church. It is our way of operating and our reason for being. Prayer has everything to do with the ability of churches to minister in their communities and in the world.

How does a church become and remain a house of prayer? The way to more focused prayer is only through fervent, persistent, pervasive, active, and systematic prayer as a priority for everyone.

Accepting God's Prayers

In the mystery of God as Trinity, God the Spirit and God the Son are continually praying to God the Father on our behalf, requesting that we have hope, the strength we need, and the vision for the journey we are walking. Paul wrote: "We do not know what we ought to pray for, but the Spirit himself intercedes for us with groans that words cannot express. . . . The Spirit intercedes for the saints in accordance with God's will" (Romans 8:26-27). In Hebrews we learn: "Because Jesus lives forever, he has a permanent priesthood. Therefore he is able to save completely those who come to God through him, because he always lives to intercede for them" (Hebrews 7:24-25). In more than two thousand years of Christian history, God has worked through people of prayer during critical points of need.

All Christians are called to imitate Jesus, who was in constant communication with God the Father through prayer. So we will keep praying. We will remain on the vine, constantly and humbly communicating with God, seeking his influence for all that we do as a community of faith. Then we may begin to stop believing that programs and strategic plans are the primary reason people are drawn to our churches. Instead we will look steadily to God as the initiator of everything beautiful and attractive about the Christian life. Our spiritual lives will grow. We will experience God's blessings as we follow his voice.

It Is Time

Although the world has changed, we see that God's desires for us have not changed. So we return to his plan for prayer in our lives.

The prayer-designed church recognizes that God surrounds us. He is working. We need to listen. It is only through this mystical encounter that we find out where, how, who, when, and why we serve. This is not about fervency or volume. It is about prayer being integral and pervasive to the practice of Christian life in the twenty-first century. It is about relationship and comprehending the purpose of prayer, and realizing that the church cannot function if we do not know how to follow God through prayer.

> *Holy God, we come to you like the disciples who came to Jesus pleading, "Teach us to pray." Some of us pray fervently and often. Some of us are hesitant. Some of us do not know how to begin. Help us cling to you like a branch clings to its vine. We desperately need you to meet us as we pray. Draw us into prayer, lead us in prayer, and answer the prayers that we breathe. In Jesus' name. Amen.*

Start Translating

1. Guide your congregation through personal reflection questions:

What one thing would you change about your prayer life? How can you make that change?

In what prayer times have you felt most connected to God? Are there methods that contribute to the depth of your experience? When do you feel least connected in prayer?

What answers to prayer have you received? Are there prayers that you consider unanswered? Why might they be unresolved?

What is your best time of day to spend time in solitude and prayer?

2. Does your church gather consistently for prayer outside of regular worship services? Consider other opportunities for incorporating prayer into the daily life of the church, starting with a fifteen-minute prayer time before each worship service.

3. Ask leaders in your church to answer the question, What are the biases or barriers that keep us from relying on prayer?

4. Send groups of three or four people on prayer walks through the neighborhood. Return to talk about experiences and observations.

5. Feature intergenerational prayer in a worship service. Include a teenager, a young adult, a middle-aged adult, and a senior adult, each praying for another generation.

6. At the onset of a service, invite people to text their prayers to a predetermined number. Share those requests during the service and invite worshipers to pray together.

7. Try a different kind of prayer. If you typically pray extemporaneously, find a book of liturgical prayers. Read the lyrics of a song or a poem to God. If you typically use others' words, try speaking from the heart, as you would to a close friend. Walk while you pray. Did these practices contribute to your experience?

8. Read one instructional book on prayer and commit to following its instruction for one month.

INTELLECTUALLY INFORMED

Staying Curious

The wisdom that comes from heaven is first of all pure; then peace-loving, considerate, submissive, full of mercy and good fruit, impartial and sincere. Peacemakers who sow in peace reap a harvest of righteousness. (James 3:17-18 TNIV)

Close-minded. Anti-intellectual. Simplistic. These are stereotypes and labels that critics have used to describe Christians—stereotypes that the church was unable to shed in much of the twentieth century and now carries forward into the twenty-first. Why? Some voices in Christianity have prided themselves in being anti-intellectual and have even regarded the rejection of deep and scholarly thinking as a virtue. Other voices are anti-intellectual by neglect. Some pastors, leaders, and Christians simply do not invest the time to be informed persons living and speaking in a world that values intellectual pursuit in a complex, cynical, and doubting culture.

Is the gospel profound, simple, and approachable to every level of intellect? Yes. Is it deeply complex and worthy of authentic exploration at theological and philosophical levels that interact with culture? Yes. Thriving churches of today will not fear the intellectual gap between straightforward and difficult. The pathway to becoming intellectually informed begins with individuals becoming more intellectually informed and then doing the hard work of expanding the process to our churches as a whole. If the church is going to translate the gospel into the twenty-first century, it can no longer afford to retreat into an easy-belief mind-set and neglect of the life of the mind.

Two Commitments for Church Leaders

Leadership formation for pastors and church leaders must be of critical concern for churches of the twenty-first century.

First, there must be a commitment to *lifelong learning*. Organizational leadership expert Peter Senge writes: "We are coming to believe that leaders are those people who 'walk ahead,' people who are genuinely committed to deep change in themselves and in their organizations. They lead through developing new skills, capabilities, and understandings. And they come from many places within an organization."[1] Pastors and leaders can reflect this idea by remaining in a continual mode of learning— mining a broad array of information, combing the church organization itself for new skills, and then synthesizing the learned capabilities and understandings.

The second commitment for a new kind of leader is to *have insatiable curiosity*. In their book *Geeks and Geezers*, Warren Bennis and Robert Thomas describe a core disposition for leaders hungering to cultivate curiosity: *neoteny*.[2] This trait is associated with what are normally considered youthful activities: curiosity, playfulness, eagerness, fearlessness, warmth, and energy. In ministry, pastors spend an inordinate amount of time wrangling through people's problems. The busyness, high expectations, and overall time demands of ministry can push pastors toward mental and emotional exhaustion. However, to grow in neoteny, pastors must fight against automated and internally focused tendencies and make room for curiosity, playfulness, and fearlessness as they explore new ministry ideation, methods, and practices.Translating Christianity into our culture and context means becoming curious and staying curious. Curiosity is a gift we already have and should be pleased to use—for its own sake and for where it can lead us. Inquisitiveness is how babies learn. It is how children gain the skills they need to survive apart from the constant monitoring of their parents. And it is one way we go beyond the first steps in our process of spiritual discovery of God and his world.

It is a great time to be curious, since we now have unprecedented access to information—a curious soul's paradise. The invention of the World Wide Web permanently ensconced us in a global information-sharing epoch. There is more data at our fingertips than any library could hold. We can watch a webcam in Istanbul. We can investigate chaos theory and grow more fascinated (or deeply confused) by it. We can search online for historical data on the Battle of the Bulge and take in new thought, always understanding the obvious—that not all Internet information is fact, just as not all words in books, newspapers, and talk-radio programs are *true*. It is easy to become hunters and gatherers of information that leads us nowhere or in the wrong direction. Internet pornography is a click away and dangerous on every level. Temptation is a different animal from curiosity. Having access to information requires spiritual maturity, personal discernment, commitment to the righteous life, and close attention to God's voice. James wrote, "The wisdom that comes from heaven is first of all pure." If you seek wisdom in intellect, seek it in purity.

God gives people an innate passion for learning. Our facile brains are tuned to the pursuit of knowledge, facts, and insight. We are hungry for it. Our tools are varied: books, periodicals, film, art, classes, lectures, readings, and learned teachers. We can search a variety of sources and read the words of great minds: scientists, philosophers, academics, writers, and theologians.

Why is this a good thing for our spiritual lives and the church? Curiosity can lead us, hungrily, to knowledge. Knowledge can lead to intellect. Intellect can lead to wisdom. And knowledge, intellect, and wisdom can be used by God to shape us, others, and culture. Sometimes God skips over the intellect stage and takes an individual straight to wisdom, but that is a special gift and should not be permission for the rest of church leaders to omit their ongoing, daily homework.

Speaking to the matter of intellect Stanley Grenz wrote: "As Christians . . . we should be concerned to gain knowledge and to hold correct doctrine in order that we might attain *wisdom* for living that we might please God throughout our lives."[3] There are plenty of people amassing depths of knowledge who are not worrying about adding the word *wise* to their résumés. But Christians must make wisdom a priority and a goal. With the mysterious aid of God we may gain the wisdom we need to discern right from wrong (not always a black and white proposition), how we should spend our limited time on earth, what we should say to whom (and what we should not say), and how we can influence our world for the better. The mind—and the church—attuned to God's wisdom can do all that and more.

A New Church Paradigm

How does the intellectually formed church function during this postmodern period? Stanley Grenz proposes that the gospel must *move beyond propositional emphasis.* Grenz writes: "A postmodern embodiment of the gospel ought not to become anti-intellectual and wholly abandon the gains of the Enlightenment. Yet the postmodern critique of modernity stands as a needed reminder that our humanity does not consist solely in our cognitive dimension."[4] The next generation, arguably the postmodern generation, seeks God by asking a different set of questions than previous generations. The modern mind tends to begin conversations by asking, "Where are the answers?" People of a postmodern mind-set begin with, "What are the questions?" They are not as interested in the four spiritual laws as much as they are seeking existential proof of God's forgiveness and salvation.

When Tim Keller came to Manhattan in 1989 New York City was not considered a prime location to start a new church. Violent crime and drug dealing were just two of the challenges confronting people coming into this urban context. Yet today, twenty years later, Keller speaks to the growing community at Redeemer Presbyterian Church in a professorial tone utilizing historical references, philosophical constructs, careful biblical exegesis, doctrinal debate, and current cultural conversations. In the beginning years Keller found the non-Christians of Manhattan amazingly curious. Keller's interest in art and music was an indispensable part of his communication. New York City is a city of many high achievers and it only made sense that a Christian pastor should be discussing ancient texts and ideas that were broader than people's current understanding. This example of a church streaming academic investigation into the Christian spiritual life shows that the life of the mind is a rewarding pursuit for believers. Churches can help their members launch beyond natural curiosity to knowledge, intellect, and wisdom. This will take energy and hard work. It may require neglect of the couch, the housework, the fitness center, and even church programming in favor of the intense discipline of learning. How can Christians—and the church—begin the task?

Stretching outside of Boxes

There is an assumption that Christian faith is tight and wrapped up, like a tiny pair of stiff shoes or a straitjacket—that living within faith hobbles the mind and restricts our curiosity. Lived correctly, the opposite is true. Paul offered prayers for the Christians in Ephesus:

> I keep asking that the God of our Lord Jesus Christ, the glorious Father, may give you the Spirit of wisdom and revelation, so that you may know him better. I pray also that the eyes of your heart may be enlightened in order that you may know the hope to which he has called you, the riches of his glorious inheritance in the saints, and his incomparably great power for us who believe. (Ephesians 1:17-19)

Paul wanted the church in Ephesus to "be filled to the measure of all the fullness of God" (3:19). These verses are just a hint at the immensity of the Creator. Even if God is unimaginable, knowing him a little more each day enlarges our minds and expands our lives.

Could God create knowledge in a person who read only the Bible? He could, of course, but *would* he? His word is the ultimate guide for our lives but is certainly not the only input. To most people he has given the intellect needed for expansive thinking in an array of areas. We should continue to discover and uncover his world and the capacity of our minds. This means cultivating a rich mind life—for his sake.

To be compelling in their world, leaders of the church in the twenty-first century should be studying materials outside their area of expertise or awareness. That might mean walking around a bookstore until they find an area they do not normally visit. Furniture design? Sociology? Classic literature? Pastors can join a book club that is made up of a variety of people who do not all think like them. They can go hear a lecture by a visiting scholar, listen to public radio, get a degree, get a second degree, and acknowledge that angry and one-sided media and politics foster close-minded postures.

This investigation will open many doors. Great poetry can expand our experience of God. Understanding how errors in judgment or moral lapses played out in history can inform how Christians make decisions today. Learning science can broaden our appreciation for creation and keep us from the foolishness of an uninformed point of view. Leaders in the American church can commit to learning, even if it is uncomfortable, and share that hunger with their congregations.

Searching the Sacred Text

Biblical scholarship is a hedge against a constricted mind. When we have thoroughly read Scripture—meditated on it and lived by it—we get a useful bird's-eye view of God working in history and in lives. We begin to understand the connection between God as he is revealed in the Old Testament and God as he is revealed in the New Testament. As we get to know him better in his complexity, we become self-conscious about simplistic views of our faith. We stop reading the Bible one-dimensionally and begin to recognize the many genres of biblical text: poetry, allegory, history, wisdom, letters, and more. We read them for their intended nuance and purpose. We stop taking verses out of context and using them inappropriately against others—as hatchets meant to wound, in defensiveness, or as platitudes. We stop feeling the need to use a single verse to refute a point of view that we disagree with.

Searching the Bible—often with the aid of trained scholars—is a key way to ground the church and ourselves in applied intellect. Paul is a powerful example of a Christian leader with an intellectual outlook. His dialogue with the Epicurean and Stoic philosophers as recorded in Acts 17:16-34 was one of the most informed, cross-cultural, missional talks recorded in Scripture. In his monologue he demonstrated understanding of religion, culture, philosophy, and context. Preachers and teachers would do well to imitate the Apostle Paul and engage in intellectual pursuits to increase the breadth of their instruction and exhortation. This is the only way that faith translation is possible for non-Christians. If you are not currently attracting non-Christians to your church building, the well-crafted teachings that integrate philosophy and broader theological conversations will serve to inform your existing congregation on how to better relate to people in their spheres of influence outside of the church building.

True Story

Jonathan is highly educated and part of a well-respected family with deep roots in the church that go back for generations. But after more than five decades attending church, he feels that he does not fit in. For the past twenty years he has "church shopped" with his family, stopping to rest every so often, but soon moving on. He is uncomfortable with the inward focus and complacency he perceives in church culture. He is impatient for change and annoyed at "conformist" behavior that he believes is sapping the intellectual integrity and potential out of the church.

"I don't want to be comfortable at church," he says. "I want to ask questions: Why do we insist on doing things this way? Why can't we change to accommodate the experiences of new generations of people who can see their way to faith but not to churches unwilling to wrestle with tough questions? What about questions that non-Christians are asking? How can the church deal with abortion other than through legislative reform? How can churches shut out certain people until they have changed their lifestyles? Why can't we ask those questions instead of dwelling on the reinforcement of previously espoused beliefs? People living in the twenty-first century as a whole don't want prescriptive answers and the immediate closing down of the discussion." Jonathan did ask tough questions like these in

---

> one of his churches and was called in to meet with the pastor, who suggested he find another place to worship.
>
> "There are going to be new questions," he says. "And we are going to be uncomfortable. People like me are looking for authenticity and relationship. I need to keep exploring what my faith looks like in action. There is dynamism in Christianity. I don't want to miss it."

Banishing Defensiveness

Mike Regele, author of *Death of the Church*, writes:

> In a world in which the field of knowledge doubles every eighteen months, the potential for a new info-bomb to reorder our basic assumptions—our paradigm of reality—is great and to be expected. A rigid commitment to an unassailable worldview, such as is typically the case in more conservative circles, increasingly runs the risk of shattering all faith—needlessly.[5]

Because some Christians have become defensive, interaction between points of view has become almost impossible. At the hint of a slight, Christians raise a cry of "Foul!" They begin rallying for the Ten Commandments to be posted in government centers or suing school districts for discrimination against their practice of faith. When they become defensive, Christians become easy to satirize and dismiss. Worse, they are perceived as bullies who have no ability to self-reflect or empathize with others.

A number of evangelical churches are beginning to rethink teaching and learning practices that unwittingly exclude groups of people. These practices are exclusionary because they contain unnecessary cultural encumbrances based upon experiences long gone. Leonard Sweet rightly states: "In a world where change is permanent, one has to be prepared to unlearn everything and begin all over again in the course of a lifetime. Leaders are constantly unlearning some things. Church culture is as much an unlearning culture as a learning culture."[6]

The rapid pace of change can and does make fools of some church leaders. For this reason, churches and their pastors, elders, boards, and other leaders are wise to prepare to unlearn and relearn in all that they do. This demands that the church seek, *along with* people who are not Christians, the realities of God. That is, for some, a shocking proposal—that non-Christians can teach Christian believers as they journey together.

Maintaining a listening and conversational attitude with people from divergent backgrounds will help pastors and leaders have a more authentic approach to learning itself. Pastor Erwin McManus believes:

> The traction comes when we become honest with ourselves and others—when we become cheerleaders for inquiry and seeking rather than simply knowing and finding. Traction comes when outsiders experience the church as a place where honest questions can be asked when people journey together to discover God and find the answer in him.[7]

The search for authentic spirituality is widespread in Western culture. There is a powerful irony in this quest because spirituality is on the rise while church attendance is in decline. Some people searching for spirituality disregard the Christian church because their experience in church buildings seems to point more to church self-importance than to God importance.

Holding honest conversations with people about the human condition requires a high level of transparency. Honesty can be ugly—and scary. Everyone struggles with sin, and most people lead shadowy lives that come nowhere close to the expectations we have for Christ followers. Bringing attention to questions and struggles in day-to-day conversations of church life can be disconcerting and even disturbing. But isn't this the ministry of Jesus?

However, just as Jesus demonstrated, honest conversations must be framed with kindness. "Loving, considerate, submissive, full of mercy and good fruit, impartial and sincere" are not characteristics we would typically ascribe to the application of intellect. How in the world do we express that kind of magnanimous spirit, and to whom? Christian thinkers glorify and illuminate God; their beneficiaries are other people.

Learning through Listening and Conversation

To attend to the development of intellect, first we listen. We are eager to share our opinions, but doing so armed with Bible verses and irrefutable facts is highly destructive to relationships and deadly to the development of a humble spirit. When we resort to preaching to people who have a different view, we use up all the oxygen in the room, which we will need to process new thoughts and engage in discourse. Listening can be difficult or even painful, but it is an opportunity to enlarge our perspective, understand another's perspective, build relationship, and come to a better understanding of issues. Hear out someone older, or younger, someone of another race or ethnic background, or someone who makes less money or more. Listening will open your imagination and your compassion for others. Remain curious about the people around you. Knowledge is gained by listening.

Conversation is a civilized and mannerly activity that does not include arguing, confronting, or forceful convicting. Philip's conversation with an Ethiopian man (Acts 8) shows how Christians can share knowledge without proselytizing by looking for openness and two-sided conversation.

Creating Scholars

Glorifying God is our primary reason for seeking knowledge—and the reason Christians should never shrink from learning. God gives the gift of great intellect to some of his people. In the past several decades these gifts have been largely underutilized.

Where have the thinkers gone? Although anecdotal evidence suggests Christians have been excluded from academia, it might be more accurate to say they have opted out. In his book *The Scandal of the Evangelical Mind*, Mark A. Noll notes: "Modern American evangelicals have failed notably in sustaining serious intellectual life."[8] A pervasive anti-intellectualism has limited and isolated Christians and removed their voices from serious discourse within the universities of America. Noll recalls respected scholars of previous centuries—John Wesley, Jonathan Edwards, Francis Asbury, Charles Hodge, Moses Stuart, George Monro Grant—who "believed in the life of the mind . . . *because* they were evangelical Christians."[9] For them, "diligent, rigorous mental activity was a way to glorify God"[10]—not the *only* way, but a significant one.

In contrast, Noll writes: "Modern evangelicals have not pursued comprehensive thinking under God or sought a mind shaped to its furthest reaches by Christian perspectives."[11] Is this a genuine crisis? Are there minds that could be fully developed for a vocation in broad scholarship? The model going forward should be of Christians who are willing to begin the hard work of building scholarship, sending some of the brightest minds into universities rather than diverting them all to seminaries. How could God use these researchers and intellectuals?

Intellect Leading to Wisdom

Deborah was an Israelite judge and prophet who lived sometime between 1380 and 1050 B.C.[12] Though the exact duties of Old Testament judges are not clear, some judges appear to have exercised legal functions while others were purely military leaders.[13] Deborah combined these two important roles while also using her God-given gift as a prophet. She was recognized as someone who served as a channel for communication between people and God. She sought God on behalf of people and provided moral, ethical, and spiritual leadership.[14]

In a world dominated by men and a culture unapologetically patriarchal, Deborah led the nation of Israel during what some consider its darkest hour. The book of Judges is the story of this violent and chaotic time. (If we were to apply the Motion Picture Association of America's movie rating to this book it would be rated somewhere between R and NC-17.) In the midst of chaos, Deborah, the only judge who was also recognized as a prophet, sought wisdom (the correct application of information to specific times and places) for the purpose of *leading people.*

Combining justice and God's wisdom, Deborah's leadership was so effective that chapter 5 of the book of Judges says that because of Deborah's leadership "the land had peace forty years" (Judges 5:31). From Deborah we learn to apply intelligence that led to wisdom, a combination of gathering information and seeking God, for the purpose of leading people. The results of such behavior: peace in the land. Remember, "the wisdom that comes from heaven is . . . peace-loving." What an interesting benefit of God-given wisdom. It can create peace.

If wisdom is the ultimate goal of an intellectually formed church, it is important to examine a key biblical figure noted for his wisdom. King Solomon in the Old Testament became almost synonymous with the word.[15] God initiated his reign as king over Israel in 970 B.C. by visiting him in a dream and making him an incredible offer: "Ask for whatever you want me to give to you."

If God came to you with the same offer, how would you respond? Wealth? Fame? Success in a career? A romantic relationship? The children's happiness and security? A toned body? Strength? Youth? Maybe Solomon considered these same options before making the famous and humble request recorded in 1 Kings 3:7-9: "I am only a little child and do not know how to carry out my duties. Your servant is here among the people you have chosen, a great people, too numerous to count or number. So give your servant a discerning heart to govern your people and to distinguish between right and wrong." God was pleased with the choice. "Since you have asked for this and not for long life or wealth for yourself, nor have asked for the death of your enemies but for discernment in administering justice, I will do what you have asked. I will give you a wise and discerning heart, so that there will never have been anyone like you, nor will there ever be" (1 Kings 3:11-12).

Solomon woke up and realized he had been dreaming, but God's promise was real. Solomon acquired God's wisdom and started his leadership strong. He served, discerned between right and wrong, made excellent decisions, wrote profound literature, built a temple considered one of the greatest wonders of the world, and with his wisdom developed an elaborate governmental system that brought him wealth and power. Then it happened. As with many people who achieve fame, notoriety, wealth, and status, Solomon began to lose focus. As his influence grew he lost sight of the purpose for his wisdom. He began to emphasize image and money. He took multiple wives as property. He grew self-important. He spent more time and money on building his palace than on the temple of worship for God. At a final breaking point he completely lost his way in hedonistic excess. He admitted as much in his own words:

> I denied myself nothing my eyes desired;
>   I refused my heart no pleasure.
> My heart took delight in all my work,
>   and this was the reward for all my labor.
> Yet when I surveyed all that my hands had done
>   and what I had toiled to achieve,
> everything was meaningless, a chasing after the wind;
>   nothing was gained under the sun. (Ecclesiastes 2:10-11)

Solomon requested wisdom and received it, but he used his wisdom to gain wealth for himself rather than to connect to the needs of people. He "went Hollywood" and his life turned into a cautionary tale rather than a heroic one. His joy turned to disillusionment, which is what happens when wisdom is connected to power and divorced from service to God. This is an important lesson for Christian leaders to remember: all learning and knowledge are to be portals to servanthood, not self-importance.

Following Jesus

Our most poignant picture of the passionate pursuit of intellect is in Jesus. He was the only person ever born who was fully human and fully God. As a human being, he needed to grow in knowledge—a mystery of God's plan. God the Father could have programmed Jesus' physical mind to know everything, like a new computer already loaded with software. But Jesus had a mind that was curious and needed to ask questions to learn and grow. While winning the favor of God he also won the approval and interest of people.

A beautiful story recorded in Luke 2:41-51 tells of Jesus, as a boy of twelve, accompanying his family on an annual ritual of travel from their hometown of Nazareth to Jerusalem to celebrate the Jewish Passover holiday. The celebration concluded and the friends and family of Jesus left Jerusalem to return home. Jesus' parents assumed that Jesus was with his friends and walked a complete day before realizing (probably at bedtime) that he was not in the traveling party. Joseph and Mary raced back to Jerusalem but could not find their boy in the bustling metropolitan city. They searched for three days. Finally they located him in the temple courts sitting among the teachers, listening and asking them questions.

Jesus' response to their frantic concern is fascinating: "Why were you searching for me? Didn't you know I had to be in my Father's house?" This was not back talk. In Jesus' mind the search for godly knowledge was natural and obvious. At twelve he already had a deep sense that he must gather wisdom. He was curious and intellectually gifted—and he knew where to go for information. Applying knowledge is an important aspect of following Jesus' example.

Being curious and gathering information is just the beginning. Jesus did not remain in the temple but did his ministry out in the world, utilizing the godly understanding he had cultivated. James emphasizes that knowledge must be connected to action: "Do not merely listen to the word [of God], and so deceive yourselves. Do what it says" (James 1:22). How is information applied to the life of the Christian?

James was probably the brother of Jesus and most certainly the leader of the early church in Jerusalem. He wrote a letter to Christians who were scattered throughout several cities:

> If you are wise and understand God's ways, prove it by living an honorable life, doing good works with the humility that comes from wisdom. But if you are bitterly jealous and there is selfish ambition in your heart, don't cover up the truth with boasting and lying. For jealousy and selfishness are not God's kind of wisdom. Such things are earthly, unspiritual, and demonic. For wherever there is jealousy and selfish ambition, there you will find disorder and evil of every kind. (James 3:13-16 NLT)

From James we learn that all of the work of attaining knowledge falls short if it is not applied to life and relationships. True Christian intellect leads to respect, humility, gentleness, sincerity, a lack of favoritism, peacefulness, mercy, good deeds, and a willingness to yield to others.

As Christians we embrace the value of staying curious, learning all that we can. We contribute wisdom and insight to our intellectually informed churches. What does the intellectually informed church look like and act like? It is a place where questions can be raised and discussed in depth without fear, where people outside of faith can be invited to be engaged and intrigued.

It is a community that is hungry to continue uncovering all the depth and complexity that the Bible has to offer. It is an environment where lively and challenging conversation takes place, where people are not satisfied with pat answers. It is a center of constant learning, like the temple where Jesus thought, investigated, and questioned.

The church is a collection of people who honor God by fully exercising the power of their minds.

> *Heavenly Father, give us a hunger to learn. As we pursue the opportunities you give to gain knowledge, may we be intellectually informed. May our desire to learn be guided into a journey toward wisdom that reflects you. When you grant wisdom, teach us how to apply it with humility. We recognize that it is never our own intelligence that ultimately matters, but rather our willingness to use your wisdom to glorify you and aid others. We make these requests in the name of Jesus. Amen.*

Start Translating

1. Guide your congregation through these personal reflection questions:

What reaction do you have to the word *intellectual*? Why?

What is God's view on the expansion of intellect? Are intellect and holiness compatible? What tensions do you see?

How have Christians neglected their intellects? Why?

In what ways do you see learning leading to wisdom in your life? Have you asked God for wisdom?

2. As a leader, spend time reflecting on the life of your mind. Determine what areas you should expand. Take a practical first step to achieve your goals of growing in wisdom. Read a book, take a class, or attend a lecture. Be willing to be uncomfortable as you wrestle with new ideas.

3. Identify respected thinkers or academics in your community. Invite them to share with your church's leadership something about their most recent writing or research project. Invite a respected university professor to speak to your church about intellectual pursuit from a Christian worldview.

4. Form a book club in the church. Include a full menu of Christian, non-Christian, and classic titles that address the current issues people in your culture are wrestling with (e.g., poverty, sexuality, immigration, and so forth). Look for opposing views and have honest, civil conversations.

5. Read Mark Noll's book *The Scandal of the Evangelical Mind* with your church leaders. Spend time discussing what you learned. From your discussion keep a list of ideas to expand your community's interest in academic development.

6. Discuss the question, "In what areas do you feel the church may be resistant to academic pursuit?" Why?

CHAPTER FOUR

COMMUNALLY FORMED

Transforming through Relationships

Jesus went up on a mountainside and called to him those he wanted, and they came to him. He appointed twelve—designating them apostles—that they might be with him and that he might send them out to preach and to have authority to drive out demons. (Mark 3:13-15)

Jesus' concept of community was countercultural even in the ancient world. He formed connections that were God focused, communal, and holistic, giving no significance to social status when that was exactly how society was ordered. He showed his followers how to live in community with one another and said that, at a minimum, they were to love others as much as they loved themselves. At a maximum, they were to lay down their lives. These startling expectations show how serious he was about the role of relationship in the life of a Christian. He chose the people and brought them together for a purpose that would only later be apparent. Had they been in charge of selecting their own traditional communities they would have missed it all.

Centuries later we are in danger of missing the unique gift of God-designed community. Our culture is market driven, segmented, and individualized. It is an assumed American value that we "have it our way." We are class conscious and often class divided. We like our experiences to be customized to our preferences. We reserve the right to pick our own like-minded friends and worship in churches that provide the resources we want, on the schedules that fit, in the style we like, with people like us. Many of us have the mobility and resources to cocoon ourselves away from people who are different.

To effectively translate our faith into this time and place requires the church to release that view of community. As Christians we are called into rich relationships—even with people we would not necessarily choose and on schedules that do not fit with our calendars. This rewarding characteristic of the faith has the potential of transforming both individuals and churches, but we are hesitant to embrace it, convincing ourselves that it is right and natural to segment our faith communities. After all, American Christians want to be with people like themselves. But in giving in to this model we are missing the supernatural power God releases into community that generously embraces his plans. The church of the twenty-first century is in the unique position of reclaiming Jesus' vision for Christian community.

Relationships of Category and Convenience

It is the same in both church and mainstream culture: our favorite communities are ones we get to fine-tune ourselves, selecting members with tender care. Our friends reflect our tastes, style, and personality. They are a good fit. They may come to us through serendipity ("She stepped on my foot in the produce aisle and couldn't stop apologizing"; "He's a Vikings fanatic, what more can I say?"), but we choose whether they get to stay in the inner circle, become pleasant acquaintances, or get politely excised. Our friends may be our polar opposites but the relationship is based on their attributes and interests, their backgrounds and availability. It is only natural.

The affinity factor has been infused into church growth philosophies. Known as the "homogeneous unit principle," this philosophy relies on attracting people to church community based upon similarities in lifestyle and socioeconomic standing. Many of the largest churches in America are ones that have successfully incorporated the homogeneous unit principle. But did Jesus intend for community to be a simple matter of personal choice?

In the church this approach can devastate God's intent for Christian community. Many of us are separated from people of different races and socioeconomic groups because this is how our neighborhoods are partitioned. We are stymied about how to reach one another even when separated by only a few miles. Our differences create giant chasms.

Once people enter the church we further partition them by placing them in age or affinity groups. Although it makes sense for people in faith communities to spend time with others who share their life stage (college, single adult, young married, thirty-somethings, seniors, and so on), we are in danger of becoming as segmented in our churches as we are in American life. When the church does not consistently and deliberately develop ways for the full community to interact in meaningful ways outside of the worship service, we begin a process of unhealthy separatism. Children go to their Sunday school classes. Parents go to their small groups. College students rarely cross paths with anyone over twenty-five. Parents with teenagers do not spend time with their elders. Elders do not spend time with children. Rather than providing an opportunity for all parts of the community to interact, the church inadvertently widens generational gaps.

Committing to Jesus

Jesus is the center of our faith communities, but he did not start out on the typical leader track. He was born into humble circumstances and should have been set for a life in the carpentry trade like his adoptive father, Joseph. Like other Jewish boys of his time, he was educated in the Hebrew Scriptures called the Torah ("Law"). He must have excelled because one of his biographers, Luke, wrote: "Jesus grew in wisdom and stature, and in favor with God and men" (Luke 2:52). But the Bible does not say that anyone knew of his divinity besides family members. Nothing is said of him becoming wealthy. Jesus lived simply. He did not begin his public ministry until age thirty. And this is how it began: Jesus invited twelve people to join him in traveling, teaching, serving, and living together.

All four of the New Testament Gospel writers describe how Jesus formed this trusted circle of disciples. Luke wrote that the night before handpicking his disciples "Jesus went out to a mountainside to pray, and spent the night praying to God" (Luke 6:12). The apostle John recorded what happened next.

> The following day John [known as John the Baptizer] was again standing with two of his disciples. As Jesus walked by, John looked at him and declared, "Look! There is the Lamb of God!" When John's two disciples heard this, they followed

Jesus. Jesus looked around and saw them following. "What do you want?" he asked them. They replied, "Rabbi" (which means "Teacher"), "where are you staying?" "Come and see," he said. It was about four o'clock in the afternoon when they went with him to the place where he was staying, and they remained with him the rest of the day. (John 1:35-39 NLT)

The community began taking shape when two men—Andrew and Simon Peter—believed John, a reliable authority, and followed Jesus. Jesus invited Philip, and Philip went to find Nathanael. This first community of Christians—although they were not called that yet—came together under the leadership of Jesus. His chosen community blended age, race, style, taste, and socioeconomic status. One author notes:

> The group . . . included a Galilean fisherman (earthy and volatile), a tax collector (servant of the governmental establishment), a fiery nationalist (renegade from the oppressed establishment), one of "untroubled faith" (Andrew), one of thoughtful reflection and prayer (John), the "doubtful" one (Thomas), and one (Judas) who eventually betrayed Jesus (Mark 3:13-18). The common bond between the twelve was only the person of Jesus himself.[1]

The Gospels recorded the constant failings, struggles, arguments, and doubts of these twelve men who followed Jesus. They were selected as disciples not because they liked one another or all got along, but because of who they would become *together*. Reading about their early missteps and disagreements does not generate immediate confidence that they were headed for future greatness, yet this unlikely collection of individuals would become the first leaders of the largest faith movement in the world's history. They were connected though their commitment to Jesus.

Does Jesus still handpick people to be in community together? Twentieth-century theologian Dietrich Bonhoeffer wrote in his classic book *Life Together*:

> We belong to one another only through and in Jesus Christ. What does this mean? It means, first, that a Christian needs others because of Jesus Christ. It means, second, that a Christian comes to others only through Jesus Christ. It means, third, that in Jesus Christ we have been chosen from eternity, accepted in time, and united for eternity.[2]

If we believe that Jesus picks the people with whom we will form community, we will have a different view of what constitutes our perfect church environment.

Becoming Disciples

In community we must become disciples rather than observers. We learn and apply the truths of Jesus so we can live a Christlike *life*.

Discipleship within community is like food preparation in a kitchen. Reading recipes or browsing pictures in cookbooks is one thing. Getting our hands onto the food, being willing to make a mess, and creating a meal is something entirely different. Learning from a master chef and working alongside her or him is the best way to internalize the craft of cooking. Jesus wants more from us than Bible reading and attendance in Sunday school classes. He wants us to follow, learn, and apply our discipleship by *doing*.

We do this together by encouraging, guiding, and praying for one another inside of community. Fellow Christians encourage us toward an always changing and maturing spiritual walk. Walt Kallestad, author of an article called "'Showtime!' No More" that appeared in *Leadership Journal*, describes this expectation arising in churches today:

> Instead of just counting the people and the offerings, now we look for evidence that people are breaking out of their private, cocooned lives and are fully engaged with God and serving him. We want them to do more than grab a cup of coffee in the lobby or meet someone new during the worship gatherings. We want them to go deep with one another. . . . In the old days, we protected people's anonymity; today we thrust them into community, doing life together.[3]

The accountability inherent in this kind of community is not a legalistic supervision but a more holistic involvement in one another's personal and spiritual lives. Becoming a follower of Jesus sets our feet on a pathway. Beyond accepting the gift of new life through a spiritual rebirth, we are called to journey with others toward a richer, deeper experience of our faith.

Building Relationships

Jesus brought people together during his life on earth and continues to do so today. *But* there are all sorts of people around us—some with big differences in attitude, history, and lifestyle. We're all supposed to get along in community? Really? How, exactly?

Here is the mystical thing: we grow by learning to live with people we would not necessarily choose. *These* friends are brought into our world by their shared desire to experience God. He can accomplish the great deed of creating harmony if we allow it. He can make these people dear to us. Sitting in a circle of prayer or serving the homeless together, you may meet people who will do anything for you: forgive you when you are dead wrong, support you through a terrifying diagnosis, anonymously ease financial pressures, and pray for you.

When the Apostle Paul wrote to fellow believers he called them "brothers and sisters," indicating that our relationships within community can be even closer than friendship. We're *related*.

What does this true community look like in the context of a healthy church?

- We act in ways that benefit others or the whole group.
- We not only embrace diversity, we proactively reach for it.
- We are authentic in roles and relationships. We tell the truth, accept responsibility, and extend grace.
- We treat one another respectfully by first assuming motives are positive.
- We go so far as to be inconvenienced in order to serve one another and the people that God has placed in our church community, living sacrificial lives.
- We listen carefully to others but speak only for ourselves.
- We pursue a standard of excellence by coming to gatherings prepared. We complete responsibilities in a timely way.
- We address disagreements and problems by speaking directly to the person with whom there is an issue, not to others, thereby stopping rumors and gossip.

If we are to nurture healthy relationships in our community we must be committed to new standards for others as well as ourselves.

True Story

The Vacation Bible School team was made up of a medley of disparate individuals. José, a newcomer to the church, was paired with Alice, who had been a member since infancy. He felt intimidated. She was in her late eighties and about as different from José as anyone could get. He felt anxious about the differences between them—not just age but, he expected, view of the world, politics, and how to "do church."

For the first couple of days he was polite but reserved. He followed directions and did his best to interact with the children who came to the program. But soon he came to appreciate Alice. She was smart, opinionated, and funny. He decided to be himself and was surprised at her acceptance of him. He had always felt that church was where people holed up with others exactly like themselves, but Alice was refreshingly different. Although he was aware of how different their life experiences had been, he saw they shared a passion for faith in Jesus. He sensed the mystical connection there and it touched him.

Talking with her between program elements, José learned that Alice had an amazing knowledge of the Bible and a generous willingness to mentor younger people. It occurred to him how unlikely it would have been for them to meet or work together in any place other than the church.

Succumbing to Transformation

This kind of community can transform us into the people Jesus wants us to be. In John's account of Jesus calling the first disciples, Jesus was "looking intently at Simon, [and] Jesus said, 'Your

name is Simon, son of John—but you will be called Cephas'
(which means "Peter")" (John 1:42 NLT). In Jewish culture, naming is a significant event.[4] Theologian Gary Burge has noted:

> Jesus is here asserting his authority over Peter and telling him
> that he is a different man, a man who is about to acquire the
> character of his true name, a name he has likely forgotten.
> [Peter means "rock."] It is striking that "rock" is not the image
> that comes through the portrait of Peter. Peter is impulsive and
> in the end will deny Jesus. But despite Peter's frailty, this name
> signals Jesus' vision for what Peter will become.[5]

Authentic, Christ-centered community leads to a moment when
Jesus looks at us and says, "I know what your identity is now, but
here is who you will be."

We are "Fearful." Jesus renames us "Courageous."

We are "Judgmental." Jesus renames us "Gracious."

We are "Lonely." Jesus renames us "Beloved."

We are "Stubborn." Jesus renames us "Accommodating."

We are "Wounded." Jesus renames us "Whole."

We are "Faithless." Jesus renames us "Believers."

As we become what he envisions us to be, our community grows
even stronger, creating a circle in which others can also be transformed. Together we are more than we are individually, because
we were created to form communities centered on Jesus.

Growing When Things Get Difficult

Let's not sentimentalize the whole idea of community.
Sometimes it is messy.

A beautifully constructed ad campaign for a camping equipment company reminded audiences of their nostalgia for camping in the great outdoors. Backed by retro footage from family home movies, the company marketed its legendary lanterns, tough tents, and timeless little green stoves by showing families from the 1960s enjoying nature and time together.

What they left out is that sometimes the kerosene lantern gasket tears or starts a fire. The mosquitoes can turn a quiet night into a bloody feeding frenzy. When setting up the tent there are sometimes not enough tent stakes and poles to do the job. Forty-five minutes into a failed set-up attempt Dad's temper finally blows: "Did you kids use the tent poles and stakes for swords and not put them back?" Mom advises the kids: "Don't talk to Daddy right now. Go get firewood." The firewood is too wet to burn because three days of rain created a small river flowing through the fire pit. And, after one hundred or more primes of the fuel can, the timeless green stove *still* does not light. Oh, you're not supposed to store the little green stove in your damp basement for eleven months of the year?

Like camping, Christian community is rewarding but also unpredictable and complex. Although it is beautiful, as God envisioned it, some days are difficult. When working, worshiping, and living alongside other fallible human beings we will experience hardship—hurt, misunderstandings, and sin. People both inside and outside the church sometimes point to these occurrences as proof that Christian fellowship does not work, that churches are full of hypocrites. Does acknowledging this truth invalidate the beauty of Christian community?

No one said there would not be difficult people. Confronted with someone we just do not like, we may eventually find ourselves reflecting on unexpected questions: "Did God bring us together for a reason? Can I learn from this experience? How can I bless this person? How would Jesus talk to him? How would he reach out to him?" Even someone who is irritating, confusing, or downright unchristian gives us an opportunity to see what God will do. Not every challenge will be removed. Inside of community there will be relationships that will not heal. But Paul wrote: "If it is possible, as far as it depends on you, live at peace with everyone" (Romans 12:18). He recognized that there are moments of stark difficulty, disagreement, and disappointment inside Christian community, but our goal should always be peace.

The Holy Spirit works inside the church. When we stand with love alongside people who are unlike us, we experience transformation. To fully experience transformational community our churches must extend themselves to people of all backgrounds and races to foster reconciliation, healing, and God's desire for openhearted community.

Getting the Balance Right

God builds Christian community. He works to hold things in balance. His ability to work will always be a mystery. And God's work has no end. Through Jesus and the power of the Holy Spirit of God people from seemingly disparate starting points can be brought into a balanced and diverse community life together. Through reconciliation to God and one another it actually works! It is a mystery though, and lives reconciled with God are always being transformed, right up to eternity.

When we feel loved in community, we want to invite others to experience it, too.

In his earthly ministry Jesus asked new people to walk with

him. Andrew was one of the twelve disciples who took Jesus' invitation to heart. Every time Andrew is mentioned in the Bible, he is bringing someone to Jesus. "The first thing Andrew did was to find his brother Simon and tell him, 'We have found the Messiah' (that is, the Christ)" (John 1:41).

Believers in the twenty-first century have this glorious opportunity to emulate Andrew. This means making real, live, caring connections with people—talking to them, getting to know them, spending time with them, inviting them into your life. This can happen in an almost endless variety of ways: through family relationships, work relationships, social networking, classes, neighbors, and impromptu connections with bank tellers, store clerks, and baristas during the day. Having an attitude of caring about the people we come across in everyday interaction changes everything.

Maybe this is a difficult switch in thinking. In the past century it was common for individuals to make a faith commitment first through large mass evangelism events and then join a community of faith. But a cultural shift has taken place. People in Western culture today are inoculated against the effects of large impersonal events. They are much more likely to join into relationships within a loving community and only later consider a commitment to faith. We must first build friendships and connect with people just as they are, wherever they are, remembering that Jesus said, "The Son of Man came to seek and to save what was lost" (Luke 19:10). We are all lost because we are imperfect and in need of God's grace. That levels the field. God's grace is an ongoing need, and Christian community is where we can profoundly experience it.

Father, as you call us into community together, we pray that you show us how to build trust and how to be gracious, forgiving, and generous with one another, even in difficulty. Break down walls of suspicion, resentment, bitterness, or apathy. We ask your Spirit to teach us how to grow beyond friendship to something richer and deeper. Let us learn from the example of your Son, who invited new people into community, embraced diversity, and loved unconditionally. Use our differences to strengthen our community. We make these requests in the name of Jesus Christ. Amen.

Start Translating

1. Guide your congregation through these personal reflection questions:

   In what ways do you sometimes feel cocooned and separated from Christian community?

   Do you remember a time when your relationships with others were a critical support to you?

   What can your church do to better foster relationships?

   What are obstacles that are keeping you from investing in deeper relationships with others? Can they be overcome?

2. Are there ways your church is isolated from the community around you, whether by choice or by circumstance? Involve your congregation in developing ways to break down those walls and call people of all different backgrounds into the church as loved and contributing participants.

3. If your church is segmented by age groups, help people reach outside their age groups through hospitality. Have each group prepare and host a meal for another group. For instance, ask the seniors to serve the young adults or the student ministries group to prepare a feast for the seniors. Consider ways that the hosting group can truly grasp hospitality (for example, selecting foods, music, and decor that fit the preferences of the group being served; *or* have the hosting group prepare *their* favorite foods). Include time for the groups to socialize, pray, or have a discussion about ways to care for one another.

4. Explore new ways of bringing people together. For instance, show a film that ends with an opportunity for people to have dialogue about the issues raised.

5. Develop new kinds of community. Form groups based on common interests, causes, or geography, rather than ones based on age or life stage.

6. Demonstrate community to people outside the church. Invite them to interact and be part of a cause that is not just a Christian concern but a human concern as well.

7. Mix up your Sunday school classes or small groups so that they are smaller than twelve. Spend at least twenty minutes or a third of class having dialogue and praying for one another. Take the risk of getting more intimate in your learning contexts.

8. Use social networking sites to bring people together. Post photos, communicate news of events, and share opportunities.

9. Create a small business-sized card to distribute to people in the church community. On one side print 1 Thessalonians 5:11: "Therefore encourage one another and build each other up." Guide participants in memorizing this verse. On the other side of the card print a simple question: "What did I do today to build community?" Invite your congregation to think about ways to invite others into their lives by caring, listening, and helping.

10. Ask that staff, pastors, and lay leaders be active in demonstrating involvement within the community—volunteering, serving in nonpastoral roles (the luncheon buffet line, the food shelf, or the decorating committee), and networking. Ask all to circulate outside of their particular area of expertise and join in the whole life of the church.

CHAPTER FIVE

COLLABORATIVELY LED

Rethinking Church Leadership

For just as each of us has one body with many members, and these members do not all have the same function, so in Christ we, though many, form one body, and each member belongs to all the others. We have different gifts, according to the grace given to each of us. (Romans 12:4-6a TNIV)

The most recent pattern of church leadership has been similar to one used in corporations for centuries. A few leaders—and sometimes just one—direct, plan, strategize, shepherd, make decisions, and attempt to fix all problems in a top-down manner. Others in the flowchart are given tasks to complete based on the decisions of these few empowered individuals.

This structure seems natural to us ministry professionals who, understandably, feel more comfortable when we have a high sense of control over what is happening in the church. Sometimes the desire for control is good and healthy because it retains order and keeps productivity rolling. The darker side of control is a wrongly emphasized use of power that restricts the gifts of others.

In both traditional corporate and church settings, leaders at the top of the flowchart perceive their work and purpose to be decision making and direction from a position of power. But, as Generation X and Millennials populate churches, the ministry leader should not perceive this role as granted de facto from an organizational chart. The hierarchical understanding of past church models will simply not work in a growing culture that does not give much importance to traditional institutional structures. Missiologist Eddie Gibbs writes:

> A sanctuary-based, pulpit-focused, and program-oriented approach to ministry means an undue emphasis on the role of the professional Christian leader. This has created a bottleneck in Christian ministry and led to the disempowerment of the laity. The professionals in ministry today have largely been trained in their seminaries, Bible schools, and Christian colleges to operate within a churched culture. Consequently, they feel most comfortable and competent when they are functioning within the institutional boundaries. . . . However, when confronted with questions, doubting, and defiant de-churched or non-churched society their professional competence quickly evaporates.[1]

We must recognize that, in the twenty-first century, the minds and hearts of diverse people working in collaboration will form ministry that works *in context*. The mission-directed church and its pastor ask, "Where has God placed us? In what time and what environment and with what people?" Then they send gifted individuals—lay or professional—into that context, with support and help, to accomplish what God has planned.

This can be frightening and uncomfortable. Translating our faith in context sometimes means dramatically changing our perception and practice of church, shifting from "how things have always been done" to new outlooks that make sense today. This may mean shaking loose some of our most closely held assumptions about leadership models of the church.

Gibbs believes that in this evolved environment what is needed is a significant shift in leadership approach—from one that controls to one that is permission giving. Consider the differences between traditional high-control churches and permission-giving churches.[2]

Traditional	**Permission-Giving**
• Narrowly focused job descriptions	• Work inspired by mission statement
• Direct and control staff and key leaders	• Equip and empower leaders
• Top-down leadership	• Relational leadership
• Information flow controlled and limited	• Information flow open and accessible
• Rewards based on seniority and loyalty	• Rewards based on skill and effectiveness

If our context has changed, we must be willing to reconsider and redesign every part of church—even its leadership structure—to be certain it is a better fit for our time and place.

Who Is Leading?

We must first shift our perception and practice of leadership in the church from pastor as sole leader and decision maker to a much more organic and holistic team approach. This church structure looks less like a pyramid and more like a living organism with parts working together in collaborative leadership to benefit the kingdom of God.

It begins with the pastor having an altered view of his or her role. The authors of *Flight of the Buffalo: Soaring to Excellence, Learning to Let Employees Lead*, describe his discovery of this new reality this way:

> For a long time, I believed the old leadership paradigm that told me that my job was to plan, organize, command, coordinate, and control. I saw my organization functioning like a herd of buffalo. . . . Buffalo are absolutely loyal followers of one leader. They do whatever the leader wants them to do, go wherever the leader wants them to go. In my company, I was head buffalo. . . . Then one day I got it. What I really wanted in the organization was a group of responsible, interdependent workers, similar to a flock of geese. . . . I could see the geese flying in their "V" formation, the leadership changing frequently, with different geese taking the lead . . . alternating as a leader, a follower, or a scout. . . . Then I saw clearly that the biggest obstacle to success was my picture of a loyal herd of buffalo waiting for me, the leader, to tell them what to do. I knew I had to change the pictures to become a different kind of leader, so everyone could become a leader.[3]

The church's familiarity with the one-pastor model is deeply entrenched, but a new understanding is emerging. This form of leadership is biblical.

> The eye cannot say to the hand, "I don't need you!" And the head cannot say to the feet, "I don't need you!" On the contrary, those parts of the body that seem to be weaker are indispensable, and the parts that we think are less honorable we treat with special honor. And the parts that are unpresentable are treated

with special modesty, while our presentable parts need no special treatment. But God has put the body together, giving greater honor to the parts that lacked it, so that there should be no division in the body, but that its parts should have equal concern for each other. If one part suffers, every part suffers with it; if one part is honored, every part rejoices with it.

Now you are the body of Christ, and each one of you is a part of it. (1 Corinthians 12:21-27 TNIV)

In a traditional reading of this passage, Christians have rightly assumed the head to be Jesus. But it is then expected that the pastor-leader initiates, supervises, and signs off on all decisions, big or small. But couldn't Jesus lead this church using gifted people working in tandem, with the lead pastor as the catalyst, coordinator, mentor, learner, and shepherd rather than traditional leader? This collaborative model does not rely on compartmentalized pastors who work in silos and report their activities to the pastoral group at large and the senior pastor in particular. It is a model of shared responsibility across lines, with generous opportunities for input and leadership.

In order to establish a new model that works in today's culture and context, we must allow our new theology of leadership to directly inform leadership practices. Pastors are leaders, but they must be willing to be equal partners with other leaders who take on responsibility and difficulties, make decisions, provide insight, and collaborate together without barriers.

Ancient Leaders, Modern Examples

We can look to the Bible for examples of this brand of leadership. Moses was one of the most powerful leaders chronicled in the Old Testament. Because of Cecil B. DeMille's epic 1956 film *The Ten Commandments* we may have a distorted view of this flawed character (that is, Charlton Heston as handsome, brave, and bass toned). But the Moses of the biblical narrative was self-conscious and hesitant. Stuck in the desert with people who had been led out of difficulty into more difficulty, Moses faced criticism on every front. The Bible recounts how people from every family wailed at the entrances of their tents. Imagine the din—and the discouragement. Moses wanted to call it quits. Sensing God's anger with how things were going, he turned the situation around so that it was God's fault:

> Why have you brought this trouble on your servant? What have I done to displease you that you put the burden of all these people on me? Did I conceive all these people? Did I give them birth? Why do you tell me to carry them in my arms, as a nurse carries an infant, to the land you promised on oath to their forefathers? Where can I get meat for all these people? They keep wailing to me, "Give us meat to eat!" I cannot carry all these people by myself; the burden is too heavy for me. If this is how you are going to treat me, put me to death right now—if I have found favor in your eyes—and do not let me face my own ruin. (Numbers 11:11-15)

If we imagine what it must have been like to be responsible for almost two million people in a desert setting we will not judge Moses harshly. Like us, he could get worn out, and when he was exhausted his weaknesses showed. How can we blame him? His leadership was being overwhelmed by the complexities of bringing an entire nation out of one of the largest empires in the world through a desert wasteland.

Instead of blasting the people—or Moses—God showed mercy and offered a practical solution.

Bring me seventy of Israel's elders who are known to you as leaders and officials among the people. Have them come to the Tent of Meeting, that they may stand there with you. I will come down and speak with you there, and I will take of the Spirit that is on you and put the Spirit on them. They will help you carry the burden of the people so that you will not have to carry it alone. (Numbers 11:16-17)

Beautiful! Three things were apparent: God had previously given Moses the gift of leadership; God heard the cry of an overwhelmed leader who needed help; and Moses was willing to imbue his chosen fellow leaders with the same gifts of leadership. These are encouraging realizations. Moses followed the Lord's directive by bringing together seventy elders at the Tent of Meeting.

Then the LORD came down in the cloud and spoke with him, and he took of the Spirit that was on him and put the Spirit on the seventy elders. When the Spirit rested on them, they prophesied, but they did not do so again.

However, two men, whose names were Eldad and Medad, had remained in the camp. They were listed among the elders, but did not go out to the Tent. Yet the Spirit also rested on them, and they prophesied in the camp. A young man ran and told Moses, "Eldad and Medad are prophesying in the camp." (Numbers 11:25-27)

Prophesying was a demonstrative form of teaching and communicating God's wisdom. Imagine a situation in which the power of God was so tangible that even the leaders who were not at the meeting were saturated with supernatural wisdom and vision.

But there was trouble.

> Joshua son of Nun, who had been Moses' aide since youth, spoke up and said, "Moses, my lord, stop them!"
>
> But Moses replied, "Are you jealous for my sake? I wish that all the LORD's people were prophets and that the LORD would put his Spirit on them!" Then Moses and the elders of Israel returned to the camp. (Numbers 11:28-30)

Joshua's desire was to control and command leadership, not to share it.

A New View of Power

Holding power loosely frees many people's gifts and enhances the pastor's availability to provide mentoring and guidance. Several people with multiple competencies can continuously acquire and appropriately apply all the leadership acumen necessary to deliver wise and comprehensive leadership in our volatile world. This is especially true in our diverse, multigenerational, twenty-first-century communities of faith.

To appreciate this truth we need to understand the time in which we live. People are not looking for the same attributes in churches as their grandparents and parents were. Their connection to church—and to faith—is no longer automatic. They need reasons to come to church—and good music, a relaxed worship style, and high-quality children's programs are not enough. We must stop expecting good preaching to draw a crowd and revitalize our congregations. (Why do we publish sermon titles on marquees and place the name of the senior pastor on the outdoor signage?) People are looking for authentic faith that changes their lives, community, and world, not consumable services and sermons.

The generations have divergent experiences and, therefore, diverse expectations that have not been well served by churches conducting church as usual. We have "improved" our offerings but we have not considered shifts in the attitudes and needs of the people around us. To accommodate younger audiences our churches may have implemented alternative worship services with moody lighting and rock music, but until we have incorporated significant and essential changes that infiltrate the whole church and leadership, we are making cosmetic alterations that will do little to transform our churches, neighborhoods, and cities. We cannot continue expecting people to come to us because of what we offer; instead, we must go to them.

Leaders in our time must be aware of these changes by including leaders who can influence the culture of the church and demonstrate the richness and authenticity of faith to new generations in a language that makes sense to them. Pastors can become catalyst conductors—men and women who work toward the full development of many individual leaders' gifts—rather than commanders and conductors. We have the opportunity to recognize and unleash the power of God through our leaders.

True Story

At the Monday worship-planning meeting, leaders from every part of the ministry staff are in attendance and the energy is electric. When the most current schedule of planned themes for preaching and worship arrive simultaneously on their laptops, everyone starts talking. The lead pastor is the host of the meeting and shares her thinking on the upcoming sermon, but she does little of the talking. She

---

is typing as fast as she can to keep up with the dialogue around the table. The conversation is barely under control.

People call out ideas for the worship experiences that will be included in the service, but they also discuss theological issues that could have bearing on the sermon writing. Everyone has something to offer and a different perspective. Verses are quoted. Teaching ideas are thrown on the table for examination and dissection. The conversation stills as everyone gathers around a laptop to watch a YouTube video called *1 to 100*. The worship arts director names possible music—from classical options to a hip-hop number. People remember Communion options that have been meaningful to them. Poetry by an up-and-coming artist is shared. There is talk of an original doxology that will be written and performed by a musician who is part of the church community. The service comes together and the meeting is over before all the creative thoughts can be shared. Everyone leaves with a list of responsibilities. The service will be the distillation of many voices and experiences. This is the kind of collaborative leadership that produces a vibrant worship experience for a diverse multigenerational community.

Best-Practice Leadership

Is this an easy transition? It will be as difficult for churches to change as it has been for the business community that has embraced this transforming wave. Within the modern corporate setting the autocratic leader is a dinosaur, an old model whose time has come and gone. An organic approach provides a timelier model for the church. Pastors should focus on strengths (their own and those of their fellow leaders), manage weaknesses, understand how other team members function as individuals, and recruit new staff to offset and balance everyone's personalities, strengths, and weaknesses.

Managing within the church can integrate some of the best practices in communities of faith and work environments today. Churches must treat employees fairly and compensate adequately. They should offer, whenever possible, off-site telecommuting options and flexibility in hours. Part-time employees should be cared for and supported. Similarly, vendors and volunteers must be valued and their time treated with respect. These are all qualities of insightful leadership.

There should be intimate and open interaction between the pastor and his or her trusted staff. It is possible that a sermon can be prepared without input, that the music people can exclusively design worship, and that outreach to young adults can be cloistered away from ministry to senior adults. But what missed opportunities! Utilizing the gifts and insights of many leaders will give us the varied understanding that we need in the years ahead. Our first task is to realign our assumptions about leadership so we create a healthy system of collaboration and shared responsibility across borders. Every staff person and volunteer leader, and their ministry areas, must see themselves fitting into the whole and continually ask what they need to do to help other areas succeed.

The Crucible of Leadership Collaboration: Worship Planning and Leading

A real test of collaboration in the church is worship design, and leaders who venture into this area together have the potential for almost immediate, dramatic results. This is not a task for the rigid or the overly sensitive, but it is critical for leaders who are willing to shape corporate worship into a more eclectic image of what our faith communities are becoming.

Collaborative leaders empower, equip, and strategically place the unpaid staff of our churches into ministry settings where they can serve with passion and excellence. Speaking polemically to this issue, Donald Miller recognized that "a sign of routinized religion is that functions previously performed by ordinary members are delegated to specifically certified professionals."[4] Launching a new worship-service style or time often requires the assistance of professional artists; however, as a church's community of quality artists grows, and volunteers make themselves available to participate in leading worship, it is critical that they be given a voice, even when they are not as proficient as a hired professional. To assign a professional to do what an unpaid staff member can and should do is to deny a church's artistic community a voice and a part in the priesthood of all believers. This is not to say that excellence should be sacrificed—or that an individual who feels "called" to singing or dramatic presentation or any other offering should be given an immediate voice. Church leaders can guide people in the development of their gifts, giving appropriate venues to appropriate people. But attention must be paid to developing the body to serve.

The Heart of a Collaborative Leader: Servanthood

The imitation of Jesus was nonnegotiable for the apostle John. He wrote: "This is how we know we are in him: Whoever claims to live in him must walk as Jesus did" (1 John 2:5b-6). Paul was also deeply concerned that Christians should have the same attitude of Christ Jesus, "who, being in very nature God, did not consider equality with God something to be grasped, but made himself nothing, taking the very nature of a servant" (Philippians 2:6-7a). If this is true, pastors must see their primary role as that of a *servant*, whether in family life, church life, or in relationships with others. They do not claim power over their families; they serve their families. They do not work for the church; they serve the church. They do not proselytize non-Christians; they serve them in the same manner as Jesus Christ so that others see and wish to experience a better way.

As a *servant* Jesus identified with people. Becoming servants will unlock new relationships and possibilities for us, too. Peter Drucker, author of *Managing the Non-profit Organization: Principles and Practices*, advises: "Developing yourself begins by serving, by striving toward an idea outside of yourself—not by leading."[5] We reach for Jesus, the creator-artist who served those he came to love.

People are searching not for figureheads who can spoon-feed them answers, but for helpers who will serve humbly alongside them. Pastors are coaches for the people of the church and their associates. Jesus never used the word *coach*, nor did the authors of Scripture. But the best leaders of the Bible were people who functioned in this role. From Shiphrah and Puah to the Hebrew midwives of Egypt, and Elijah to Elisha as his prophetic successor, coaches are people who embody the ideals that they represent. They teach, equip, and lead others into the same ideals. Leaders "model the defining characteristics of their ministry that they want to inspire within every facet of their ministry."[6] As coaches, pastors are critically concerned about positioning others for success and utilizing every resource within their influence to help others discover their role in the kingdom of God—all while working with them toward collective goals.

Who Is with Me?

Perichoresis is an ancient Greek word that literally means "circle dance." George Cladis spoke about this word and its implication in the church when he wrote: "Based on the biblical descriptions of Father, Son, and Spirit, John depicted the three persons of the Trinity in a circle. A *perichoretic* image of the Trinity is that of the three persons of God in a constant movement in a circle that implies intimacy, equality, unity yet distinction, and love."[7] This is a stunning image of how God has designed all relationships to work, especially within the context of Christian community. Miroslav Volf writes that God is "not a self-closed unity, but rather a community of the three divine persons. Believing in this God—surrendering one's existence to this God—necessarily means entering into the divine community. . . . Trinitarian faith accordingly means becoming community."[8] The image of God's relationship with himself can become our model for relationships and interactions with others. With this *perichoretic* perspective on relationships we see people with more open, loving, and egalitarian eyes.

Like Jesus, whose whole ministry focused on reconciliation, we take a *healing attitude*. Paul spoke about God's desire for reconciliation:

> Therefore, if anyone is in Christ, the new creation has come:
> The old has gone, the new is here! All this is from God, who
> reconciled us to himself through Christ and gave us the min
> istry of reconciliation: that God was reconciling the world to
> himself in Christ, not counting people's sins against them.
> And he has committed to us the message of reconciliation.
> (2 Corinthians 5:17-19 TNIV)

Reconciliation with God is both a one-time event (salvation) and an ongoing event (sanctification). Our reconciliation with one another is similar. We can decide we will reconcile with others and then meet each day with the openness to do so. The complex dynamics of relationships requires us to stay open so we can heal hurts, work out differences, and come to agreement or peace.

One of the attributes of Christian leaders, then, is *helping hands*. The Apostle Paul wrote in Philippians 2:3-4: "Do nothing out of selfish ambition or vain conceit, but in humility consider others better than yourselves. Each of you should look not only to your own interests, but also to the interests of others." When we are actively looking to the interests of others we are given opportunities on a macrolevel—assisting others in fulfilling their broader life purpose—and on a microlevel when they simply need help. In the old model of CEO pastor this may be nearly impossible because of the workload inherent in this role, or undesirable because of the image required by such a position.

How Do We Lead?

The church is not buildings or places where people gather for worship, but the community of all believers. The church is built by God himself and is Christ's presence on the earth today through the power of the Holy Spirit (Matthew 16:18; Acts 2:47; 1 Corinthians 12:12-27). This belief guides our practice of equipping people for shared ministry and pursuing the empowerment of the Holy Spirit in all activities of the church.

The church is both visible and invisible. The visible church gathers for worship, ministry, the sacraments, and other activities that honor God and invite people to commune with him. The invisible church is the true church as God sees it in the hearts of his believers (2 Timothy 2:19; Hebrews 12:23). D. R. W. Wood has written: "The kingdom of heaven or kingdom of God is the central theme of Jesus' preaching, according to the Synoptic Gospels."[9] It is the responsibility of the church to be a witness of the kingdom of God (Matthew 24:14) and carry out the ministry of Jesus (Matthew 10:8; Luke 10:17).

The days of unilateral church are over. The complexity of changing communication models, the evolving cultural diversity of our congregations, and the explosion of artistic eclecticism in worship mandates that leaders form collaborating teams to accomplish their work. David Straus echoed this when he wrote: "With good process, people can generate more creative and comprehensive solutions collaboratively than they can by themselves."[10] Love is the connecting feature, signified and sealed through covenant and commitment. This is not a casual connection. It is biblical and Spirit led. Our goal in collaboration is also to reflect the image of God and engage people in practices of godly interaction. By forming community the church realizes the visible and invisible church and builds the kingdom of God.

Picture of the New Leadership

Paul described life in the Christian community as body life.

> The body is a unit, though it is made up of many parts; and though all its parts are many, they form one body. So it is with Christ. For we were all baptized by one Spirit into one body— whether Jews or Greeks, slave or free—and we were all given the one Spirit to drink.
>
> Now the body is not made up of one part but of many. If the foot should say, "Because I am not a hand, I do not belong to the body," it would not for that reason cease to be part of the body. And if the ear should say, "Because I am not an eye, I do not belong to the body," it would not for that reason cease to be part of the body. If the whole body were an eye, where would the sense of hearing be? If the whole body were an ear, where would the sense of smell be? But in fact God has arranged the parts in the body, every one of them, just as he wanted them to be. If they were all one part, where would the body be? As it is, there are many parts, but one body. (1 Corinthians 12:12-20)

Paul used a clever metaphor, as strange and as mystical as it was, to talk about a group of people functioning like a human body. The body is a complex unity of organ systems that integrates the various parts of our bodies. So, we have circulatory, digestive, immune, reproductive, and several other systems that are all inter-connected to keep our physical being in balance and functioning healthfully. The body of Christ functions at its peak when there is value given to all parts.

When one system or part of the body is missing, damaged, or not functioning properly, the whole body is out of balance. It might even die. Those churches that believe they will attract a crowd with an outstanding pastor for young adults without making certain their ministry to elderly adults is fully functioning will be stunted. A fabulous choir does not replace the need for direct, ongoing spiritual formation. A burgeoning number of small Bible groups will not replace the integral function of service to the poor or marginalized. Without prayer even the most vibrant worship service will languish.

Likewise, a broad reading of the Bible tells us that the complete body of Christ is diverse. It includes people with different gifts and abilities, but also people from every culture, socioeconomic level, and stage of life. Keeping this balance is harder than people think. Forces of racism, ageism, sexism, and selfishness dismember and dissect Christian body life. Churches have fallen to these forces.

To live out what Paul exhorts in 1 Corinthians 12 requires us to constantly ask ourselves: Do we have young, middle-aged, and older people present? Women and men, girls and boys? Poor, middle-income, and rich people? Multiple skin colors and backgrounds? Are our voices divergent and representative of our global community? If we do not see a complete body when we look around we must be determined to rehabilitate the body to health by actively seeking and welcoming those who are missing.

Acceptance is our essential glue. The Apostle Paul concluded his 1 Corinthians 12 conversation on body life with the words: "And now I will show you the most excellent way." Anyone who has attended a church wedding has heard what Paul wrote next. Known as one of the greatest descriptions of love ever penned, 1 Corinthians 13 drives home the point that everything the body of Christ does is useless if love is not the primary motivation and expression. People getting married need to hear this important message, but the original audience of Paul's love chapter was the whole body of Christ. Love and acceptance are the only adhesives that can bring together and hold together a diverse group of people. The risk in using glue is that it gets sticky. The reward is that people glued together by God form a complex mosaic of beauty that transcends the typical one-dimensional existence we often limit and sequester ourselves into.

Harnessing the Will to Change

This is a tall order. We must ask ourselves, Even if it is desirable to change, is it possible?

It is a matter of will. We act in alignment with our beliefs. People who believe they have a chance to win the lottery will risk losing money to do so. If, as Christians, we believe that God has the power to physically heal people, we will pray for healing. Pastors who believe their job is to command and control the church will work with all their might to do so. Conversely, those who view the work of God's kingdom as a shared responsibility will focus their attention on equipping others for collaborative ministry, creating not just programmatic leadership but shared and equal responsibility to organize, implement, and oversee.

Whether we are one or one hundred years old God has brought us together to work collaboratively as the church. In this perfected church our hierarchy is deactivated. Our biases are obliterated. We view all contributors—paid, unpaid, full time, part time, leaders, staff, vendors, visitors—as integral and therefore precious. That is the beginning of full health in church leadership.

Holy God, we struggle to allow you to lead us. We want you to inspire our view of leadership, a view focused on grace. We want you to transform our relationships into holy reflections of your love and acceptance. Give us new eyes. Teach us how to be a collaborative community that is faithful, passionate, and vibrant. Provide direction and empowerment through your Holy Spirit, inspiration and perspective from your word, and leadership by Jesus' model. Amen.

Start Translating

1. Guide your congregation through these personal reflection questions:

   Do you recall a time in your life when someone invited you to share in leadership responsibilities?

   Was it a positive or negative experience? Why?

   What can be done to foster greater leadership sharing and development in your church?

2. How can your congregation become a welcoming community to people who might not ordinarily be invited into the church? What ideas could those people bring to worship planning and other ministry areas? How can we involve new voices in creating the church?

3. Foster collaboration in sermon and worship preparation. Plan a monthly creative meeting in which you look at worship services a couple of months ahead. Give everyone the

sermon synopsis and planning content ahead of time so they can bring ideas to share.

4. Organize a teaching team at your church. Include a variety of pastors, whether staff or special guests. Get together quarterly. Talk about possible ways to improve and change.

5. Encourage church leaders to network with other organizations and civic leaders. What can the church learn from businesses and other agencies?

6. Read Numbers 11:10-17, 24-30. Keep a journal of creative ways in which the church can do a better job nurturing leadership, sharing, and developing the church.

7. Consider revamping your corporate flowchart. Redraw relationships in a more organic form. How can responsibilities and decision making be redistributed?

8. Identify people in your community who bring gifts that have not been utilized in the development of your church. Think about ways you can include their gifts in ongoing ideation.

ARTISTICALLY INFUSED

Joining God's Creative Impulse

Then the LORD said to Moses, "See, I have chosen Bezalel son of Uri, the son of Hur, of the tribe of Judah, and I have filled him with the Spirit of God, with wisdom, with understanding, with knowledge and with all kinds of skills—to make artistic designs for work in gold, silver and bronze, to cut and set stones, to work in wood, and to engage in all kinds of crafts." (Exodus 31:1-5 TNIV)

The arts have always been a voice of commentary on culture and a definer of culture. But in the Protestant tradition full expression of the arts has been stifled for several centuries. This can be traced back to the Reformers' overzealous purging of the arts from the Protestant worship experience. As a result of this historical transition, Christians—particularly evangelical Christians—have not routinely experienced varied forms of artistic expression and, therefore, have not embraced theater, literature, dance, film, painting, or sculpture in the church or in their lives. But that is changing. Many churches are now moving beyond previously held misconceptions and are experiencing a renaissance of the arts in all parts of church life. Christians are embracing new forms of art to expand their understanding, touch their culture, and create ethereal and concrete works that communicate mystical realities. As artistic expressions enhance worship and the practice of faith, they are expanding our abilities to communicate meaning. They are growing our communities through participation and experience.

A Culture Leaning toward Creativity

Observers and writers note that right-brain thinkers have become the new leaders in the corporate world. It is no longer only the linear, sequential, left-brained person who is heading corporations or leading businesses into the future. It is now the creative thinker who is more agile, more adaptive, and able to thrive in rapidly changing circumstances. Books such as *Rise of the Creative Class* (Richard Florida) and *A Whole New Mind: Why Right-Brainers Will Rule the Future* (Daniel Pink) paint a portrait of this new world. We are in a culture of imagination, connectivity, and accelerated change. It is a dynamic and destabilizing globalization. This is like creation on steroids.

This reality has implications for the translation of the Christian faith. If people of our culture view creativity as a natural pathway to truth and meaning, the church must be proficient in sharing the truth and beauty of faith and grace through artistic expressions. And that means embracing the artist.

What Kind of Artistry in Worship?

Most of us define worship by the standards of our personal experience and traditions rather than by a broader examination of the biblical foundations of worship. The Bible offers a broad framework or theology for worship but no prescription for the style or philosophy with which every Christian church must create worship. Where in the Bible can we find exhortations to use or not use organs, drums, video clips, violins, or electric guitars? Where in the Bible are we commanded to include or not include announcements, drama, responsive reading, or expository preaching? The Bible does have a lot to say about worship and provides a vital groundwork for worship in our congregational life.

Scene One: Creator God

"In the beginning God created. . . ."

God's first action on behalf of humans is recorded in those first five words in Genesis. God embarked on a design process that human beings will forever strive to comprehend. How he did it is less important than why he did it. Love and creativity mingled as God designed light; separated light from darkness; imagined planets into existence; placed atmospheres, earth, air, water, land, and plant life; and created the first animals.

Then "God created human beings in his own image, in the image of God he created them; male and female he created them" (Genesis 1:27 TNIV). This idea of beings made in the image of God captivated people of faith from the beginning. The ancient Hebrews phrased it *tzelem elohim*, and the early church coined the phrase in Latin, *Imago Dei*. It means that human beings share some of the attributes of God. We have independent thinking, reasoning, and emotional capacities. We have moral and spiritual attributes. And, like God, we are creative.

The Bible is filled with remarkable accounts of what people did with these God-given creative impulses. Christian author Gary Thomas describes it this way:

> From Genesis through Revelation—people worshipped God in many ways: Abraham had a religious bent, building altars everywhere he went. Moses and Elijah revealed an activist's streak in their various confrontations with forces of evil and their conversations with God. David celebrated God with an enthusiastic style of worship, while his son, Solomon, expressed his love for God by offering generous sacrifices. Ezekiel and John described loud and colorful images of God, stunning in sensuous brilliance.[1]

And there are other examples. Miriam played a tambourine and danced (Exodus 15). David played musical instruments and designed elaborate musical experiences in worship. Lesser-known artists Bezalel and Oholiab were craftsmen who designed three-dimensional objects used in the early worship tabernacle (Exodus 31). Isaiah and many other prophets acted out intense dramatic scenes to communicate their prophetic messages symbolically (Isaiah 20). Jesus spoke in story form using analogies to bring truth to life. The people of the early church etched murals on catacomb walls.

Our understanding and use of the arts in worship and in life can be traced throughout historical periods of the church. What do we learn about God's view of artistry, and what can we take forward into the future?

Scene Two: Arts in Early Worship

Abraham and the patriarchs lived a nomadic existence. While they traveled, however, they fashioned altars and made offerings and sacrifices to God. These were theatrical practices demonstrating God's ownership of all things. We are never to come to worship empty-handed.

God next instituted feasts, festivals, and specific rituals in worship: the Passover feast (Exodus 12); commitment to the law (Exodus 20); new places of worship, ordination of priests, and sacred holidays and assemblies (Exodus 25-33; Leviticus; Numbers). The directive of God to Moses was, "Get involved," "Worship in meaningful ways," and "Don't remain a spectator."

After the Exodus and Joshua, worship fell into disrepair. As king of Israel David reorganized the worshiping community and initiated several changes. Instrumental music, round-the-clock worship leaders in the place of worship, nonsacrificial worship, and focus on the presence of God in the peoples' midst came to the fore. Passion and purity in worship drove David to a deeper experience of God.

Solomon dedicated the completed temple in all its grandeur to God. Then things started going wrong. Solomon lost his connection to God. Somehow the temple began to be regarded as a reflection of his own glory. Inappropriate influences, lack of God's vision, and poor decisions led to the destruction of the temple and the downfall of the nation of Israel.

The absence of the temple and homeland caused the faithful of Israel to find ways to worship in their new surroundings. Their faith was renewed. The local synagogue began to be the center of worship, community, and learning. Homes, also, were gathering places for followers of God. The people's ability to find faith in the midst of exile and suffering teaches us to be certain that worship finds its way into our homes and communities.

Early Christians used the synagogue model to start, but quickly began to form distinct elements for their worship. Jesus became the center of all present expressions and the focus of future hopes and dreams. There was a continual adaptation of the existing worship elements into innovative forms. First Timothy 3:1-13 describes new literature and writings, new organizational forms, and the emergence of creedal statements. These worshipers remind us to ask if we, too, are continually shaping our worship with Jesus as the center.

Scene Three: The Christian Church

Biblical history ended with the completion of the book of Revelation (A.D. 96) and the death of the apostle John (A.D. 98). However, the story of Christian worship continued to be written through three major eras.

The centuries immediately following biblical history feature the Christian mass as the primary form of corporate worship. The persecution of Christians in the second and third centuries forced many to worship in secrecy. When Christianity moved from the shadows of persecution into the limelight of state religion in the fourth century, several aspects of the worship liturgy changed. In a position of significant power and influence the Christian church developed a more fixed form of the mass. The idea of worship as a mystery was in sync with the teachings of Jesus in Matthew 18:20 and 28:20. But the institutional church lost its way in key areas, amassing power, distancing worshipers from understanding worship, and claiming that participation in mass amounted to personal salvation. The arts were perceived as receiving undue focus. The resulting excesses were among the elements Reformers set out to purge.

In 1517, the Protestant Reformation began sweeping through Europe. Its work was to simplify and purify the Christian faith, and it did so with stunning clarity and efficiency. Yet, it was an imperfect process. One consequence was the almost total removal of the arts from the Christian community. Some now consider this removal to be collateral damage—the arts wiped out because of guilt by association with specific abuses of the church rather than because they impeded the practice of the Christian faith. The Reformation was principally a reform of theology. However, it was inevitable that new theological beliefs would have a major impact on existing worship forms.

The Free Church tradition, originating with the Anabaptists and English Puritans, followed Ulrich Zwingli's emphasis on the word only. The Anabaptists and other emerging Free Church traditions refused to allow any form of worship that could not be substantiated by Scripture. This included the use of various instruments, dance, vestments, and more.

The twentieth century represents one of the most accelerated periods of change in modern history. Contrary to its promises, the mechanistic, rationalistic, and empirical approach of the Enlightenment had not made the world a better place. Movements of thought ranging from quantum physics to New Age religion challenged the Enlightenment's presuppositions and created a breeding ground for multiple forms of spirituality, a focus on the supernatural, and the rediscovery of mystery. Within the Protestant tradition six identifiable streams developed: formal-liturgical worship, traditional hymn-based worship, contemporary music-driven worship, charismatic worship, blended worship, and emerging worship.

There are many lessons to be learned from biblical history and Christian tradition. The early church development of the mass with an emphasis on mystery teaches us the importance of understanding what we believe and the urgency of creating systems to express those beliefs. However, we have to note that devastating consequences ensue when church leaders use those systems of belief to create hierarchies and thus diminish the involvement of people in the act of worship. The Reformation period teaches us the importance of the word of God and our personal acquisition of faith and salvation. However, stripping corporate worship of visual beauty, symbolic richness, and liturgical depth can influence congregations to become overly focused on the performance of preachers and musicians. Twentieth-century history of worship teaches us that human philosophies are frail and transient, but God, who never changes, faithfully reveals himself to every generation in new ways. It is time to reimagine worship practices for the twenty-first century.

Scene Four: An Arts Renaissance

In the church, we have missed the arts. We have been poorer for their scarcity not only because they would have added thoughtfulness and reflection to our gatherings, but also because they could have added eloquence to our expressions of love for God and opportunities for outpourings of our God-given creativity.

Thank God for their return. After a centuries-long drought churches are rethinking the place of the arts in the experience of faith. A maturation and redemption has taken place. As the church rediscovers and reconnects with all types of thoughtful and meaningful creative expressions, we are entering a new period of renewal and vibrancy.

David Kinnaman notes in his book *UnChristian* that new generations of believers and potential believers "relish mystery, uncertainty, and ambiguity."[2] The arts are a primary way of articulating that sense of mystery and providing glimpses of insight.

Christian thinkers and leaders are moving away from the assumption that all creative art forms except music are suspect or at least inconsequential. Instead, they are seeing new and ancient arts as a pathway to deep, meaningful worship, spiritual transformation, and compelling outreach. Underway is a poignant return to the biblical narrative in which we approach artistic expression as a creative gift from God designed to honor him and reflect his existence in our lives.

Times change, artists change, and so does their art. Change is inexorable, but that is good. Art forms and their multiple expressions are simply the means by which we communicate with one another, God, and people around us. Our expressions are temporal and often linked to what God is doing at a particular moment in time.

This constant movement and change creates a challenge. How does a Christian community of diverse people embrace the voices and expressions of all present generations? The church falls into quicksand when it designates specific styles or art forms, usually linked to personal taste and generational preference, as more sacred than others. The healthiest, most dynamic congregations continue to reshape the worship experience—and the Christian experience—so multiple generations can learn, communicate, and experience God. Is it possible for the church to avoid segmentation and bitterness over issues of style?

It is—but only with mutual love, respect, courage, willingness to learn, and selflessness. There will be conflicts as we try to embrace the diversity of Christians of every age and background; but we can comfort one another, knowing that this struggle is nothing new. Every generation must face new expressions of faith that innovators, artists, or younger worshipers bring to the church. We can learn to value multiple forms and styles, holding to biblical principles while recognizing that people find meaningful worship in different ways. The music of young musicians energizes and inspires. Ancient artwork reminds us of our connection with historical figures, whether heroic or flawed. Great old hymns— sung or spoken—can aid in contemplation. Skillful dramatic elements help us see our struggles and ourselves in the context of God's world and plan. There are no decrees in the Bible regarding the use of organs, drums, cellos, or electric guitars, so we use them all. There are no exhortations to use or not use drama, the Christian liturgical calendar, expository or narrative preaching, art on large display screens, film, or other forms of worship. The church has appropriately looked at the whole biblical narrative for broad principles of the arts in worship.

We must also leave behind the notion of a less-than-full integration of the arts in worship and daily life. The arts are not decoration, "specials," or add-ons to worship, reflection, prayer, or study. Creative narrative, music, painting, and sculpture are worship in themselves and can be as integral as preaching and prayer. They are one potent way of learning and discovering. In that sense, a worship gathering of Christians is organic and should not be bound by expectation of where art "fits" and how people interact with it. God offers numerous resources to be woven into our experience of him.

The Written Word

Robert Browning said, "God is the perfect poet." God is the Creator, the source of all beauty and imagination. He is the Word.

When we look closely at the language and images of the Bible, we see complex, literary construction as well as overt themes. Scripture represents a collection of voices, styles, and formats that say God uses the power of words, expertly and imaginatively woven, to speak to people. Similarly, people use poetry to speak to God and fellow humans. It is interesting how much of the Bible is devoted to poetry. Roughly 30 percent of this sacred collection of works is written in poetic form.

Many people have a poor understanding of poetry and little experience with high-quality work. Doggerel is rhyming verse that is trite and forced, comfortable and pat. By contrast, literary poetry delves into important subjects and is skillfully constructed. Poetry can be evocative, imaginative, or even uncomfortable. It always makes the reader or listener think and feel. Poet Paul Engle defined poetry this way: "Poetry is ordinary language raised to the nth power. Poetry is boned with ideas, nerved and blooded with emotions, all held together by the delicate, tough skin of words."[3] Writing poetry—or listening to, reading, memorizing, or reciting it—can be an act of worship and another way to experience God.

In the church we have much to discover about the written word and its place in faith. Rather than forcing our writings into the form of exhortation, we can also share grace, worship, and our deepest questions through fiction, theatrical experiences, and written prayers. Whether in blogs or articles, drama or prayer, word artists will contribute to our communities as they ask questions and seek answers from God.

All Kinds of Music

Music has been a strong part of the practice of Christian faith. Most believers are comfortable participating in hymn singing and other forms of music.

Isaac Watts, born in 1674 in Southampton, England, wrote more than 750 hymns. Many consider his work "When I Survey the Wondrous Cross" to be the greatest hymn ever written.

> Were the whole realm of nature mine,
> that were an offering far too small;
> love so amazing, so divine,
> demands my soul, my life, my all.
> (*United Methodist Hymnal*, 298)

Today, the tune and sentiments expressed still resonate with many people, but we would not think of them as cutting edge. In his time, however, Watts was considered a revolutionary—a radical churchman—who produced the contemporary music of his time. Prior to his hymns, music in the church was limited to the poetry of the Bible as designated by John Calvin, the sixteenth-century Reformation leader. Watts wrote hymns from a first-person perspective, bringing together broad theological ideas and, for the first time, personal application and response. Some people wanted to silence him. It is fortunate that there were openhearted Christians who saw the value in his art. He paved the way for a new flock of Christian composers and poets.

Classical music used to be the pop music of Western culture. Composers such as Bach, Handel, Purcell, Mozart, Beethoven, Wagner, and Strauss were the rock star celebrities of their day, bringing controversy, intrigue, and sometimes scandal to their roles. Throughout the Renaissance and the baroque, classical, romantic, and modern historical periods, the church explored what we now call classical music because it was the cultural language of the day.

God continues to shape new artists of faith. Twenty-first-century musicians, composers, and vocalists bring rich faith, experience, experimentation, emotion, and research to their work. They embody a new sound and a new experience for the worshiper while also reflecting the thoughts and experiences of the artist. We need to continue to encourage artists to create and share their work.

This is a tough transition for some people in the church, mostly because we are apt to like what we like and be unimpressed with—and even disdainful of—new modes of expression. We are human and sometimes inflexible. But our desire to enjoy styles that are familiar must be balanced with a deeper desire to draw others into community. We must keep growing and learning. This challenge calls for great tenderness on the part of church leaders and worshipers alike. Each generation can be submissive to others, allowing for the freedom of all to experience God in worship.

Although new music may sound strange or irreverent to the ears of some, we know that God is still inspiring and informing the minds of people he has gifted.

Dance for Joy

The poet W. H. Auden wrote: "I know nothing except what everyone knows—if there when Grace dances, I should dance."[4] He was speaking metaphorically, but grace *is* a compelling reason for dancers to dance. Read the Bible and see King David dance and lead others in dance before God and God's people (2 Samuel 6:14). Psalm 149 exhorts God's people to "praise his name with dancing" (Psalm 149:3). Even in David's time dance could be met with opposition by people who did not understand. King David "and the entire house of Israel" were bringing the ark of the Lord to Jerusalem "with shouts and the sound of trumpets" (2 Samuel 6:15). Worshiping, David danced. His wife Michal watched from a window, disgusted. When he returned home she reproached him sarcastically: "How the king of Israel has distinguished himself today, disrobing in the sight of the slave girls of his servants as any vulgar fellow would!" (2 Samuel 6:20).

David defended his actions.

> It was before the LORD, who chose me rather than your father or anyone from his house when he appointed me ruler over the LORD's people Israel—I will celebrate before the LORD. I will become even more undignified than this, and I will be humiliated in my own eyes. But by these slave girls you spoke of, I will be held in honor. (2 Samuel 6:21-22)

You may not be familiar with dance; you may not be able to dance; but in worship you can experience dance that honors God and leads others to a worshipful moment. Every church will need to sort out how dance can be incorporated in the life of the church in its time and place. There was no question that King David made some people uncomfortable with his ecstatic display of dancing. Dance is an art form that requires strength, skill, planning, and thought. Congregations have begun to experiment with choreographed forms of dance to create a moment of illustration or reflection.

Embracing Visual Arts

Whatever the medium, visual art "has power to translate emotions and intellect into form . . . power to express personal and community beliefs and values through concrete symbols . . . power to transform—to change one's vision, quality of life, and life circumstances."[5] Artists can reflect the beauty and message of God, give voice to the collective voice of the congregation, and connect to the needs of the community.

To build their confidence and trust, Christians need opportunities to view and learn about different forms of art. Drawings, paintings, animation, mixed media, or installation art can be an amalgam of color, movement, concept, and story. Film weaves narrative, music, image, and technology. Sculpture conveys spatial textures and forms. Textiles offer a palette of color, patterns, scenes, and forms. Church architecture can reflect high or low symbols of theological meaning. Photography can invent imaginative scenes or crop and capture poignant or thoughtful moments of real life.

Artists in the church community can create works for screens, sanctuary displays, worship guides, booklets, and events. They can give lessons. They can lead tours of local museums and galleries so participants can view a variety of styles and media from different art periods. They can help break down the barriers of distrust and fear by helping people contrast biblical art, historical portraits, fine ceramics, sculpture, and contemporary art. They can give permission for viewers to be open and inquisitive even when viewers do not immediately understand what a particular piece is about. They can assist as fellow Christians learn how to discover context and meaning within the art they view.

123

Our churches can become centers for visual arts. A gallery space in the building can become a place for retreat and reflection as well as a location to draw people from outside the church. Together we can lose our fear of visual arts or the expectation that all art must represent literal spiritual matters in order to speak to our hearts or faith. Visual art, in whatever form, should make us react, think, feel, and worship.

True Story

The artist was accustomed to the lack of attention to her paintings but still felt disappointed. Art was part of history, part of culture, part of life—and an integral and essential aspect of *her*. She was curious as to why her work did not interest people in at least investigating further. Her fellow artist friends came to her gallery exhibits but she did not have much support among people from church, even when the subject matter was faith related. Art was the way she worked out her feelings and confusion about life on this planet. She did not have all the answers but she felt that she was relatively skilled at expressing the questions. Her faith was integral to her work. Sometimes she felt isolated from both of her communities—artists and other Christians.

She was not asked questions, but once she tried to speak of her passion for painting to someone at church. She got one of those looks that seemed to say her "hobby" was nice but nonessential. She suspected, because of comments she had overheard about "modern art," that people were uncomfortable when they did not immediately understand the

---

meaning of an artistic work. She would have enjoyed talking about this topic, but so far no one had expressed interest.

She picked up one of her smaller canvases and looked at it, feeling the ridges of paint beneath her thumbs. Life's hard stuff was here. She also saw the ineffable beauty of God's involvement in her sometimes pitiful, sometimes exquisite, mostly hopeful life. She loved to paint that contrast—grasping the sliver of loveliness between two worlds. It was her praise song. She longed for a community where she could share that praise with others.

Exploration and Transformation

Inside the diverse community of Christian artists one thing is true. They are people of hope.

For the person of faith there is always the hope of transformation through the gospel of Jesus—a reality that is never Pollyanna-ish, simplistic, or overly moralistic, yet is tangible. Having hope does not mean that we do not struggle with doubt. It does not mean that we do not sometimes despair at the cruelties of poverty, war, disease, and natural disasters. But whatever the realities, artists of faith ultimately believe that humans have the power, through God, to intervene. A writer may explore a hopeless or depraved character, but always underneath is the overarching hope that restoration and redemption are possible. A painter may paint the ugliness of poverty but maintain the hope that people can respond with help.

Some artists probe their understanding of beauty in God's world. What is it? Can it be found only in the idyllic settings of nature, or can it also exist in the mundane, the unexpected, and the random? As Christians, we do not need to be afraid of these explorations.

Creating an Artistic Church for the Future

When the church distanced itself from the arts it also pulled away from full engagement with artists. A resurgence of the arts will attract the creative minds of writers, dancers, photographers, filmmakers, sculptors, and textile artists back into the circle of faith. As we move into the future our artwork will begin to be reflexive with the community around us. As we connect more and more to the people and neighborhoods around our churches, artistic expressions will begin to draw others to the church. Consider one young person's story.

A college student studying theater at a local university took voice lessons from an accomplished instructor at a prestigious nearby theater. They discovered their mutual faith and developed a friendship.

When her church needed a volunteer skilled in dramatic Scripture reading, the instructor hesitantly asked the student if he would be willing to give it a try. He was anxious to gain experience and intrigued with the idea of using his gifts within the church. There were several dramatic elements over the next few weeks, and he agreed to rehearse and present.

Soon he considered the church his home and the community his friends. The members of the congregation were astonished by how much his voice and expression added to their experience of worship.

Because the arts are ways that individual Christians serve, a revitalized focus on them will offer artists opportunities to be intimately connected and to contribute to their faith communities.

Some individuals in your congregation may feel devoid of creative skills. Perhaps their brains are far more left than right. They can still experience the arts in relation to faith. They can gain inspiration from people who possess the gift of creativity. Songs can be illustrated. Worship can be danced. Prayers can be thoughtfully composed. Scripture can be dramatically interpreted. The community of faith will join in the arts and help most in the congregation experience the story of God and the unfolding reality of Christian life together.

At the peak of their effectiveness the creative arts lead us to make deeper commitments by inviting us to stretch our limited understanding of God. Great and enduring art will continue to restore and feed people in coming centuries. Sometimes a song, sculpture, poem, sermon, or painting will be lost and then reemerge as it connects with a new generation. In the meantime, the artists of our past and the gifted artists of our present can help spur and encourage worship and spiritual transformation in a language that intrigues and inspires.

Leaders can be conduits, helping to infuse the artistry of God into individual lives and the collective life of the church. Our expressions of love for the ultimate creator will profoundly speak to the people in our culture and context.

Creative God of the universe, we are grateful to have some small part of your creativity dwelling within us to reflect you. We are inspired by your unfathomable imagination. Like David, we lay our creativity before you as a sacrifice of love and honor for you. Let us use your artistic gifts to form community with

one another and share your message of hope. We pray this in
Jesus' name. Amen.

Start Translating

1. Guide your congregation through these personal reflection
   questions:

   How have the arts been used in the life of the churches that
   you have attended?

   What new forms of art would you like to see in the life of
   the church? In worship services?

   How could the arts be used more in our church to help both
   Christians worship more effectively and non-Christians
   understand in the Christian message?

2. Design a worship experience around God's creative activities and characteristics. Make it a discipline to incorporate
   new forms and styles of art in the day-to-day life of the
   church.

3. At a local coffee shop host a poetry event based on a spiritual or faith-related theme. Invite people to read their original work or poems they have discovered in publications or
   anthologies.

4. Ask an artist to come talk about how faith influences his or
   her work. Invite the participation and ideation of your

church community's artists through focus groups or informal meetings.

5. Invite or hire an artist-in-residence from any discipline to contribute to or influence worship planning for a year.

6. Consider and discuss God's viewpoint on the creative arts based on these passages of Scripture: 1 Chronicles 15:1–16:6, Psalm 150 (music), Exodus 15:19-21 (dancing), Exodus 31:1-11 (visual arts), Isaiah 20 (drama), and Matthew 13:34-35 (storytelling).

7. Pray for the artists in your community. Ask God to enhance your experience of worship through many different art forms.

8. Visit local arts venues— theaters, museums, galleries, or readings. Spend time afterward discussing what you experienced and observed. Consider partnering with a local arts organization to host a special event.

CHAPTER SEVEN

MISSION MINDED

Risking Love

Just as you sent me into the world, I am sending them into the world. (John 17:18 NLT)

Listen to the conversations in your church after worship and you are likely to hear lively discussions about the sermon, the music, favorite sports teams, the weather, restaurants, children, jobs, movies, trips, politics . . . . What about mission? Even with desperation in our neighborhoods, cities, nation, and world, it seems that a pervasive sense of love and mission has receded from our consciousness. Are we struggling to ignite the imagination of our congregations, painfully aware of how much work there is to be done with never enough resources?

Mission—the willingness to open the doors of the tent to others—has become, for some, like a vitamin pill. We know it is good for us and we take our nutrition, but many Christians do not long for it or seek it. Mission may be relegated to a committee that meets on Tuesday nights, or celebrated with an annual event. When individuals planning short-term mission trips approach parishioners, many are happy to write a check. There are photographs of church-supported missionaries on the missions wall. But the church has yet to inspire every member of the church to see himself or herself as a full participant in carrying out the mission of offering the grace of Jesus with love and gentleness every day.

An ancient-modern Christian ethos is emerging, one that brings a sense of openness to mission and a reconnection with our own personal roles in the work of Jesus. To be thoroughly and passionately mission minded is one important way the American church will be able to translate Christianity in our time and place. But before we can become mission minded, we must discard our baggage about the nature of the effort and realign the church to mission, acknowledging what mission is and who can participate.

Realignment #1: Embrace the Mountaintop Proclamation

Jesus' mission directive was delivered at the end of his work on earth and recorded in the writings of Matthew. Jesus brought his disciples together on a mountaintop in Galilee one last time and gave them instructions and reassurance that would shape their lives: "All authority in heaven and on earth has been given to me. Therefore go and make disciples of all nations, baptizing them in the name of the Father and of the Son and of the Holy Spirit, and teaching them to obey everything I have commanded you. And surely I am with you always, to the very end of the age" (Matthew 28:18-20). This was a profound proclamation, one of Jesus' core teachings.

When we comb through the Gospels we will find no clarifying reference to indicate that some followers go and others do something else. To those of us calling ourselves Christians, Jesus said, "Go. Everyone. Take on this mission." It is good and right that churches encourage, pray for, and financially support people who are called to full-time vocational ministry. Yet, when Jesus called his followers to share in his work, he never suggested that the rest of us should assume our individual calls could be fulfilled vicariously through the lives of professionals.

That's a hard truth for some believers who face the prospect of sharing personal faith with dread. We have turned mission into "evangelizing," an activity that sounds like it is based in an attitude of superiority. No wonder we hate this sort of one-sided proselytizing, protesting, "I'm terrible at evangelizing. I have obligations to my children, my career, my church. Whenever I talk about my faith I get the cold shoulder—or hostile rejection! People more gifted than me should be doing this important work. We already give to missions!" The objections of Christians are compelling and real, but they do not for a moment change what Jesus requested when he said those words. He never intended for his followers to fear or dislike the idea of telling their story, or for the church to send missionaries but not also equip its people to go and share locally.

Perhaps the disciples brought baggage with them to that mountaintop, too—the baggage of self-doubt. They had strength when Jesus was with them, but imagine the reality of going back to town and stirring up the still-smoldering resentment of the religious leaders. Go and tell people that the man who had been so violently executed really *was* the Messiah promised to the Jews? Oh, sure. Brilliant idea.

But they had been steadily prepared for this moment, and Jesus had always given them the ability to accomplish the responsibilities he put before them. Perhaps they now remembered the words of their rabbi and leader who had prayed with them the night of his arrest:

> [Father,] now I am coming to you. I told them many things while I was with them in this world so they would be filled with my joy. I have given them your word. . . . I'm not asking you to take them out of the world, but to keep them safe from the evil one. . . . Just as you sent me into the world, I am sending them into the world. (John 17:13-18 NLT)

Like the disciples, we must start by being willing to hear Jesus and by embracing his words as serious and timeless, trusting that Jesus has relevance in our culture.

Realignment #2: Know Your Context

Missiologists are quick to point out that the work of defining a church's missional context requires a thorough process that touches the entire identity of the church itself. In *The Missional Church in Context*, theologian Craig Van Gelder outlines seven aptitudes that churches should consider when fully defining their context.[1]

1. Churches must learn to read their sociological and theological setting.
2. They must anticipate that church forms and methods will be, by necessity, created by and for the contexts. (This occurred for the New Testament church as the gospel was contextualized into the Hellenistic world at Antioch.)

3. They must anticipate reciprocity. (The group that has shared the gospel is changed by those who have received it.)
4. Churches must understand that they are particular. (Churches and their contexts are continually changing and must be regularly reviewed and discerned.)
5. They must understand that ministry is always practical. (The practice of ministry is always normalized by Scripture but must reflect the patterns and shape of the culture in which a congregation is ministering.)
6. They must understand that doing theology always depends on one's perspective. Theologians Stanley Grenz and John Franke discussed this aptitude when they wrote:

> Yet, while acknowledging the significance of *sola scriptura* as establishing the principle that canonical Scripture is the *norma normans non normata* (the norm with no norm over it), it is also true that in another sense *scriptura* is never *sola*. Scripture does not stand alone as the sole source in the task of theological construction or as the sole basis on which the Christian faith has developed historically. Rather, Scripture functions in an ongoing and dynamic relationship with the Christian tradition, as well as with the cultural milieu from which particular readings of the text emerge.[2]

This is a call to recognize that although theology begins with Scripture, its veracity is fully embodied in the crucibles of tradition and context.

7. Churches must understand that organization is always provisional. The way churches organize must be adaptive and flexible as they continually take context and culture into consideration. Denominationally affiliated churches are

wise to treat polity as guiding principles and not prescribed practices. The specific organizational practices of a rural church in Pella, Iowa, are not going to work in suburban Miami, Florida.

Christian churches in America must take on this task of self-evaluation in order to speak effectively to their communities.

Realignment #3: Mesh Cultures

The people in the early church grew and thrived because they were willing to live in the messiness of combining people from different nations and tribes under the umbrella of the reconciling love of Jesus Christ. To invite new disciples, the apostles of Jesus crossed cultural lines that had never before been breached. Jews and Gentiles worshiping together? Eating together? Paul wrote about the effort and dedication it took to speak across cultural lines.

Though I am free and belong to no man, I make myself a slave to everyone, to win as many as possible. To the Jews I became like a Jew, to win the Jews. To those under the law I became like one under the law (though I myself am not under the law), so as to win those under the law. To those not having the law I became like one not having the law (though I am not free from God's law but am under Christ's law), so as to win those not having the law. To the weak I became weak, to win the weak. I have become all things to all men so that by all possible means I might save some. I do all this for the sake of the gospel, that I may share in its blessings. (1 Corinthians 9:19-23)

Jesus will place us, even today, into communities of faith that break down human divisions—if we are willing to hear his call and follow his lead.

Redeveloping Christian mission in our increasingly diverse American setting means that majority-culture Christians must learn from and work alongside people of many races and cultures. That means inviting nonwhites into leadership and sacrificing certain assumptions in order to understand Jesus Christ through multicultural lenses. We may not immediately know what that means or looks like. White Christians will have much to learn as the American church humbly reaches out to voices of diversity to ascertain pathways forward. This is an urgent imperative. Pastor and professor Soong-Chan Rah states, "If you are a white Christian wanting to be a missionary in this day and age, and you have never had a nonwhite mentor, then you will not be a missionary. You will be a colonialist. Instead of taking the gospel message into the world, you will take an Americanized version of the gospel."[3] The church cannot afford the cost of an ethnocentric gospel.

Going all the way back to the beginning of the Christian church, the work of converging all people around the redemptive work of Jesus Christ was difficult. The development of our congregations' mission in this time will also feel chaotic and disorienting at times. But as more people in the church become engaged, there will be a transformative effect. The very culture, character, and DNA of our churches will be reborn. Our communities will be challenged and encouraged as they see the fruit of God's work through them.

Realignment #4: Reach Out in the Manner of Jesus

Evangelism is difficult for many of us because we prefer that others not wear religion on their sleeves. We get fidgety when asked to listen to someone else's beliefs. We have uncomfortable memories of Bible bangers whose screechy fervor drowned out the voices of others and demonstrated a complete lack of humble self-reflection or understanding.

The church is learning that if we are sensitive to the mission of Jesus we are not called to accost strangers, hand out tracts, or deliver eloquent monologues that make people convert on the spot.

Jesus said we are to go into our world "in the same manner" that God the Father sent Jesus the Son. What does that mean? In what manner did God send Jesus? Part of the answer can be founded in John 4. This is where we see Jesus demonstrate a simple yet profound method of sharing faith. "[Jesus] left Judea and returned to Galilee. He had to go through Samaria on the way" (vv. 3-4 NLT). Jesus took a risk. Many Jews, particularly the very religious ones, never traveled through Samaria; instead they journeyed east to Jericho on a desert road from Jerusalem and then up the Jordan Valley. Jesus made the decision to leave the familiar highway and encounter people underserved by the religious leaders of the time.

Samaritans were longtime enemies of the Jews. In 722 B.C., the king of Assyria forced the Samaritans to settle in northern Israel. The Jews disliked the Samaritans because they had a history of combining traditional Jewish worship of God with idols and non-Judeo practices. There were many rifts over land and holy sites, with violent encounters between Judean Jews and Samaritans. Jesus chose to walk a path where people did not expect his kindness.

> Eventually he came to the Samaritan village of Sychar, near the field that Jacob gave to his son Joseph. Jacob's well was there; and Jesus, tired from the long walk, sat wearily beside the well about noontime. Soon a Samaritan woman came to draw water, and Jesus said to her, "Please give me a drink." He was alone at the time because his disciples had gone into the village to buy some food. (John 4:5-8 NLT)

Jesus took another risk by speaking to a Samaritan woman. He conversed with her as an equal.

> The woman was surprised, for Jews refuse to have anything to do with Samaritans. She said to Jesus, "You are a Jew, and I am a Samaritan woman. Why are you asking me for a drink?"
> Jesus replied, "If you only knew the gift God has for you and who you are speaking to, you would ask me, and I would give you living water." (vv. 9-10 NLT)

Missing the metaphor, the woman pointed out that he had no rope or bucket for drawing water. She wondered aloud if Jesus thought he was greater than Jacob "who gave us this well."

> Jesus replied, "Anyone who drinks this water will soon become thirsty again. But those who drink the water I give will never be thirsty again. It becomes a fresh, bubbling spring within them, giving them eternal life."
> "Please, sir," the woman said, "give me this water! Then I'll never be thirsty again, and I won't have to come here to get water."
> "Go and get your husband," Jesus told her.

"I don't have a husband," the woman replied.

Jesus said, "You're right! You don't have a husband—for you have had five husbands, and you aren't even married to the man you're living with now. You certainly spoke the truth!" (vv. 12-19 NLT)

Now she was intrigued and asked him a theological question. He picked up on her interest and segued into topics of great spiritual importance.

"The time is coming—indeed it's here now—when true worshipers will worship the Father in spirit and in truth. The Father is looking for those who will worship him that way. For God is Spirit, so those who worship him must worship in spirit and in truth."

The woman said, "I know the Messiah is coming—the one who is called Christ. When he comes, he will explain everything to us."

Then Jesus told her, "I AM the Messiah!" (vv. 23-26 NLT)

This sounds like a good conversation, with plenty of natural and lively interaction. Jesus wasn't doing all the talking. He was listening, too. Imagine the relief, surprise, and gratitude this woman must have felt when she was treated kindly rather than with the usual contempt. "Just then his disciples came back. They were shocked to find him talking to a woman, but none of them had the nerve to ask, 'What do you want with her?' or 'Why are you talking to her?'" (v. 27 NLT).

In a simple but dramatic display, Jesus showed his disciples how to treat others, even those they considered lower in status. This was a "show, don't tell" occasion that would have a dramatic effect on whoever witnessed the interaction. The woman was not sure if this man was the Messiah, but she was excited enough to run and gather others in the village. Notice that Jesus waited for her to return. Taking time was one of the ways he connected with people. Giving time is a simple thing, but essential—and more powerful than we realize. An electrified crowd formed. Many people believed after that encounter. The woman had become a catalyst for belief.

Through this experience, Jesus taught his disciples how to carry out simple grace and friendship; but the story is recorded in the Bible for our sakes, too. What do we learn from it?

Jesus built a bridge through simple conversation. He asked the woman at the well for a favor: "Please give me a drink" (John 4:7b NLT). This might seem like an insignificant request, but by asking this woman for help he demonstrated his acceptance of her. He understood and was willing to care about her exactly for who she was at that moment in time—*before* she made changes in her life and even if she *never* made changes. Engaging in other people's lives must be motivated by love.

The awkward term "friendship evangelism" has emerged to describe Christians sharing their faith through friendship rather than through preaching. The phrase itself shows a difficult balance. The evangelism part can weigh too much ("I'm really here to win you over to my side"), or the friendship part can become the focus ("I'm a Christian, but my faith is not something I talk about or demonstrate in any of my actions"). "Friendship evangelism" sounds like a program rather than a natural way of living and caring for people. As Christians we should love making new friends, and people who spend time with us will know that our faith in Jesus is central to our thinking, actions, and purpose. Having a healthy and active spiritual life is key to this occurring without strain. Like Jesus we are to care for people without ulterior motives.

So here is where Jesus' directive becomes real for the church. He does not require Christians to leave home each day planning to evangelize everyone they meet. Instead, he asks them to love the people in their lives. To accomplish this purpose he will shape our circumstances to give opportunities for friendships with the people around us. Honest, authentic friendships occur during the normal stuff of life. Getting water from a well. Sharing a meal. Going to a ball game. Standing in line. Taking a class together. Going to the mailbox at the same time. This is just as true for pastors. While we proclaim the good news in our churches, our most effective opportunities for sharing will occur through natural and loving interactions with people who may or may not enter the church.

True Story

A woman struck up a conversation with her landscaping professional after noticing a cross tattoo on his arm.

"Are you a Christian?" she asked.

"No." His answer was blunt and his face set. "My life is too busy. I don't have time for religion."

She nodded, commiserating with the feeling of being overbooked.

"But—"

She had a moment of discomfort, not wanting to press into the man's personal life. Then she gathered a degree of courage and continued.

"But when I see a cross I think more about relationship than religion." He hadn't shut her off yet, so she went further. "A lot of people think Christianity is about church, but it's really about transformation and growing a spiritual relationship with Jesus."

"No time, no interest." Skepticism and bitterness were in his expression.

The conversation moved on to other topics. The woman did not feel any need to push harder. Her impulse was not to badger or bully the man. She wondered why he seemed angry about church. As they talked, she felt herself warm to him. He was a no-nonsense person who told the truth. She was glad she had been brave, realizing that he couldn't know that the Christian life was about joy and not religion if she didn't share what she had experienced. Maybe they would get a chance to talk again. Maybe he would see something in her kindness and actions. Who knew where future dialogue might lead? Only God.

Our cultural context makes sharing grace thorny. As the chasm between mainline culture and church culture widens, so, often, does the gap in understanding between non-Christians and Christians. Compounding the difficulty has been the strange and devastating blending of Christianity with American politics. Today someone asked to describe a Christian is much more likely to mention political affiliations than love and service. Some people have claimed the name of Jesus to argue their side of divisive issues. Full of misdirected conviction, they have had shouting matches with their "opponents," demonstrating a lack of compassion for others. Jesus shouted in anger only at hypocritical *religious* leaders—the people of faith who used their power and reputation to look good and lord it over others. Time after time, the approach that Jesus took with people who did not have faith was to listen and speak with them.

Does anyone want to be harangued into following someone else's convictions? We cannot and should not attempt to rule people's behavior or attitudes by force or self-righteous pronouncements. Honestly sharing the meaning and message of Jesus obligates us to love others the way Jesus did.

It is time for the church to call all Christians to a purified mission, one that follows the footsteps of Jesus.

Realignment #5: Service = Universal Love

Some people have a unique gift of evangelism. They are uniquely empowered by the Spirit of God to share the good news of Jesus and thereby change lives. But each member of the Christian community is also called. The church can help people stop thinking so much about what they say and help them know that sharing good news begins with what they do. For this enormous task of sharing good news, what has God given his followers besides the relentless sense that they should be doing more? He has given them the ability to love.

Serving is what Jesus was always about. Ongoing, integrated service as part of church life is essential. In *The Externally Focused Church*, Rick Rusaw and Eric Swanson write:

> Service is the only location that encompasses the needs and dreams of the city, the mandates and desires of God, and the calling and capacity of the church. Service is the "sweet spot" where all three come together. Service is something the community needs, God desires, and the church has the capacity to do. The community may not care much about salvation, but it does have needs. It is in meeting those needs through service that meaningful relationships develop, and out of relationships

come endless opportunities to share the love of Christ and the gospel of salvation.[4]

God brought Jesus to Samaria, and he has placed us where we should be, too. Some people will devote their lives to full-time missions, working in countries (including America) where there are overwhelming needs. That vocation could mean teaching school, building houses, providing medical services to patients with HIV/AIDS, giving microloans to impoverished people to start small businesses in their communities, training church leaders, or any number of other missional efforts. For the rest of us, we may be exactly where we need to be, but we need to remind ourselves of our purpose.

Realignment #6: Humbly Understanding Truth

Jesus was ready to speak of spiritual matters when they came up. In a short period of time, Jesus and the Samaritan woman had a spirited dialogue about wells, spiritual growth, ancestor history, and her life. This is how conversations can go with people who are spiritually hungry. You start out talking about a drink of water and end up dipping into significant issues of faith and life. There came a point where Jesus spoke the truth boldly. At the perfect moment, he got to the point: "I AM the Messiah!"

The word *truth* is a loaded word, giving rise to the complicated question, Is there such a thing as truth anymore?

In nineteenth- and twentieth-century philosophy and theology, people understood that genuine truth was an empirical construct to be discovered, established, and understood. This notion is rooted in the eighteenth century and the historical period known as the Enlightenment, a period when philosophers and theologians built elaborate systems of thought that sought to clearly define objective reality. Truth discovered through rational thought was a normative goal of many people regardless of faith belief systems. The "modern" viewpoint of the Enlightenment collapsed over the course of the twentieth century when people in Western culture became disillusioned with systems that promised to answer all of life's questions but did not deliver. In reaction, people of today have adopted a postmodern perspective, strongly pursuing an understanding of truth as relative to their personal experience, believing that their improvisational constructs of reality will offer more than prescribed truth.

But nearly everyone recognizes that without at least some understanding of truth, all of society would collapse without rule of law, a sense of moral values, and sound judgment. Christians recognize that Jesus talked about truth and even referred to himself as "truth." We cannot simply go with the flow of relativism, but rather must grapple with what Jesus meant when he called himself "truth." In conversations, it is critical that we humbly acknowledge the complexities of defining truth. We must realize that any arrogant assumption that Christians own or have all truth figured out and wrapped up is wrong. We learn daily about truth through our relationship with Jesus.

The Gospel writer John reported a story about a famous rabbi named Nicodemus who came to Jesus one night to talk. Nicodemus probably feared that association with this controversial teacher would cost him his influential role as a member of the Sanhedrin (the Jewish ruling council) and a part of the prominent religious group called the Pharisees. Jesus referred to him as

"Israel's teacher"—not *a* teacher, but *the* teacher of Israel. Nicodemus had vast knowledge, but he was unprepared for the teachings of Jesus, which were intriguing but shocking and subversive to traditional assumptions. Most alarming to the religious leaders was the authority and boldness with which Jesus taught. Three times during their conversation, Jesus said to Nicodemus, "I tell you the truth." "I tell you the truth, no one can see the kingdom of God unless he is born again" (John 3:3). "I tell you the truth, no one can enter the kingdom of God unless he is born of water and the Spirit" (John 3:5). "I tell you the truth, we speak of what we know, and we testify to what we have seen, but still you people do not accept our testimony" (John 3:11). These were bold and confrontational statements.

Nicodemus questioned these truth statements because he did not understand Jesus' metaphor for conversion. "How can an old man go back into his mother's womb and be born again?" (John 3:4 NLT).

The metaphor Jesus used was new birth, but the need for new birth was centered on vision: Jesus said, "No one can see the kingdom of God without being born again" (John 3:3 TNIV). Human beings are born spiritually blind and unable to see God. Some people are *completely* blind to God and others have, at best, blurred or dim ideas of who God is. Regardless of what they do— think good thoughts, live good lives—they remain incapable of clear spiritual vision. John summarized this human dilemma and God's solution with these words:

> For God so loved the world that he gave his one and only Son, that whoever believes in him shall not perish but have eternal life. For God did not send his Son into the world to condemn the world, but to save the world through him. Whoever believes

in him is not condemned, but whoever does not believe stands
condemned already because he has not believed in the name of
God's one and only Son. (John 3:16-18)

These verses contain the gospel, the good news, of Jesus Christ.
This is the "aha" moment in the teaching, the "aha" moment of
the Christian faith. When Jesus, the Son of God, came at that time
and at that place, he was God's specific answer for the reconciliation of humanity to himself. John summarized the cosmic problem and its answer: we are all broken and condemned because of
our sin; Jesus came to save, not accuse; it was out of God's intense
love for the world that he sent Jesus to create a path for reconciliation with God.

For two thousand years the church has grappled with the
meaning of this deceptively simple truth, and it has lost its
focus at times: during the dark years of the inquisitions,
throughout the miserable premise and cruel enactment of the
Crusades, and amid rigid twentieth- and twenty-first-century
theopolitics. But the gospel message is not about forcing or
proselytizing others to think and act like Christians. Rather the
unleashed gospel of Jesus Christ is an explicit global expression of God's love inviting everyone to life. And the Bible
teaches that we need a conversion, a change in thinking and in
heart, to be able to see God.

The Evangelical Dictionary of Theology describes conversion
this way:

> We do not procure salvation, but we decide for salvation once
> our inward eyes are opened to its reality. Conversion is the sign
> but not the condition of our justification, whose sole source is
> the free unconditional grace of God.

Conversion is both an event and a process. It signifies the action of the Holy Spirit upon us by which we are moved to respond to Jesus Christ in faith. It also includes the continuing work of the Holy Spirit within us purifying us of discord and contumacy [which means stubbornness], remolding us in the image of Christ.[5]

The message of reconciliation with God is what Jesus wanted his disciples—us—to share. It is the call and mission of every Christian to live out this invitation. This call requires the church to shift from the traditional missions program to an environment in which everyone is called—and in which everyone understands that what he or she offers mission is not an "in" to an exclusive Christian club but the beginning of a spiritual relationship and reconciliation with God.

God has a generous way of solving problems and getting Christians back on the path. He prepares his people to answer the call, and he does not require eloquence, a photographic memory of the Bible, or airfare to Katmandu. In fact, God has always done his greatest work with people uniquely *un*prepared to accomplish the tasks he presents.

We must have courage. We are in good company with two millennia of people God has used to spread his grace and love to every continent of the world.

Heavenly Father, we want to be sent like Jesus was sent. Like the disciples, we are sometimes unsure of our abilities to effectively answer Jesus' call. Give us courage to risk, the desire to be genuine, the patience to listen, the selflessness to serve, and faith that shines a light on you, not us. Help us feature the love of Jesus in everything. We struggle with self-consciousness and fear, but we hunger to imitate you. Teach us how to choose your pathway. In Jesus' name. Amen.

Start Translating

1. Guide your congregation through these personal reflection questions:

   When God calls you to missions, what is your reaction?

   What specific fears do you have about sharing your faith?

   What are some tough questions that people may ask you about your belief in Jesus?

   How well is your church doing acts of service to bless the surrounding community?

2. Identify one of your financially supported missionaries who could be a catalyst for new hands-on work with your church. How can you engage him or her as an adjunct ministry staff member or coach to your congregation? Consider inviting him or her to relocate to your neighborhood to accomplish ministry, teach, and mentor your congregation for an extended period of time.

3. Define a strategic project that a missionary could organize and orchestrate to involve people from your congregation.

4. Form a task team to assess possible partnerships with non-profit organizations in your neighborhood. Formulate a discernment process as a partnership path to long-term relationships. For example, plan six to twelve months of

short one-time joint projects to see how you work together. Have conversations about the vision, mission, and theological belief systems of both organizations. Talk through possible scenarios that could go wrong. Talk about how money is going to be utilized. Schedule interaction between your ministry staffs.

5. Invite a leader from a ministry organization to be interviewed in your worship service.

6. Ask leaders to discuss what your church is doing to equip people to share their faith with others. Brainstorm ideas to create a broader understanding of mission, culture, and context.

7. Invite a team of church leaders to make a list of the largest obstacles keeping people from experiencing a relationship with God. How can these obstacles be overcome? Spend time praying that God will help you find ways to remove obstacles and share love through tangible acts of service.

CHAPTER EIGHT

SOCIALLY AWARE

Seeking Justice for Everyone

Blessed are they who maintain justice,
who constantly do what is right. (Psalm 106:3)

In a world filled with injustice, the socially aware church puts flesh on the Christian claim to love our neighbors. Christians hoping to translate their faith to make it resonate in our culture will pursue individual and systemic justice for others, even at personal expense.

Justice is "the establishment or determination of rights according to the rules of law or equity"; "the quality of being just, impartial, or fair"; "the principle or ideal of just dealing or right action"; "righteousness"; "conformity to truth"; "correctness."[1] Social justice is "the distribution of advantages and disadvantages within a society."[2] It is much more than compassion; it is compassion's result. When we see injustice we are moved by compassion and act to bring justice to an individual or group of people who are underserved, undervalued, disenfranchised, powerless, or poor. The Bible instructs: "Let justice roll on like a river, righteousness like a never-failing stream!" (Amos 5:24).

Just-minded Christians are aware of the people around them. They seek to stop injustice by changing culture, laws, practices, and policies that discriminate, intimidate, and oppress. They attempt to balance systems of inequity to the point of forsaking themselves and their own rights.

This is important because God's justice is pure, impartial, and perfect, an ideal that we can constantly pursue and never achieve. But how beautiful to always seek it, to help the church become the embodiment of justice on earth. Practically speaking, this means growing so sensitive to injustice around us that we are irresistibly drawn to intervene for good whenever we see inequity, unfairness, or suffering.

Sacrificial—and Like Jesus

In this century, justice may be one of the most life-giving outreach imperatives for people of Christian faith. Social justice is a reflection of Jesus, who, through the Incarnation, gave up everything to advocate for humanity and compels us to do the same. The church must go beyond *believing* in the justice of Christ to actually *living* it.

Has the church been underemphasizing a biblical imperative?

Mae Elise Cannon, author of *Social Justice Handbook: Small Steps for a Better World*, argues that modern evangelicals have stressed "personal righteousness and piety" but have "missed much of the intended meaning bursting through the Scriptures about justice. It is critical to understand that righteousness and justice are interconnected in both Testaments."[3] She adds that the Greek word *dikaios*, which appears in the New Testament, has many meanings, including:

the observation of right laws, keeping the commandments of God, being virtuous, righteousness or justice. . . . In the New Testment, *dikaios* refers to both Old Testament ideas—justice and righteousness. The King James Version translates the word *dikaios* thirty-three times as being "just" and forty-one times as "righteous." However, other English translations typically translate this word as "righteousness" and not "justice." . . . A lot has been lost from their original languages to English.[4]

The following are examples of New Testament verses that include variations of the word *dikaios*, with the word *justice* added to demonstrate a fuller and more accurate meaning: "It is proper for us to do this to fulfill all righteousness [and justice]" (Matthew 3:15); "Blessed are those who hunger and thirst for righteousness [and justice]" (Matthew 5:6); "For in the gospel a righteousness [and justice] from God is revealed" (Romans 1:17); "As it is written: 'They have scattered abroad their gifts to the poor; their righteousness [and justice] endures forever" (2 Corinthians 9:9 TNIV).

Realigning righteousness with justice may change how we approach the social justice issues before us.

Distracted by Wealth

To serve well, we must identify with the needs of marginalized or oppressed people. This is a complex task in a culture that allows not only the achievement of basic needs but also the generous accumulation of goods and wealth. An uncomfortable reality for the American church is its relative comfort. Can we, in a world of epidemic slavery, oppression, and poverty, truly serve from a position of privilege afforded us by the circumstances of our birth?

The work of social justice mandates that we dilute our positions of privilege and our expectations of security. ("When my mortgage/retirement/children's college tuition is taken care of, then I will attend to the needs of the poor.") It is only in a position of vulnerability that we begin to understand what much of the world faces each day for survival. We are called not to pity, but to understanding and action.

People of the church will face the difficulty of disciplining themselves to seek humility regardless of any personal achievements or wealth. Robert D. Lupton, author of *Compassion, Justice, and the Christian Life: Rethinking Ministry to the Poor*, writes:

> It is disquieting to realize how little value I attribute to "the least of these," the ones deemed by our Lord to be "great in the Kingdom" (Matt. 5:19, NIV). I have viewed them as weak ones waiting to be rescued, not bearers of divine treasures. The dominance of my giving overshadows and stifles the rich endowments that the Creator has invested in those I have considered destitute. I selectively ignore that the moneyed, empowered, learned ones will enter this Kingdom with enormous difficulty.
>
> One who would be a leader, I am cautioned, has a greater weight of responsibility to honor the despised, share his earthly possessions, model interdependency and encourage the use of gifts concealed in the unlikeliest among us. To the leader, when the gift of humility is offered, the gift is the salvation of the proud, which comes with great difficulty from learning to receive from those who are the least on Earth, yet greatest in the Kingdom.[5]

So the gift of wealth is a dangerous one—one that we must handle with respect and a degree of fear. To some of us monetary wealth is a tremendous opportunity to bless others. To others of us it will always be a barricade between God and us and the passionate pursuit of righteousness and justice (*dikaios*).

People in rural Mozambique, one of the poorest countries in the world, have no savings accounts or social safety nets to catch them when they are desperate. They have the church. Community volunteers from the local faith communities visit people dying of AIDS and bring comfort and prayer. There are no Bible study materials. There is no medicine to treat malaria or HIV/AIDS, no food bank, and often no church building. What the church does have is prayer and Christian service. The church *is* the local justice. This is the identity the Christian church in America should always be striving for with God's help.

Diverted by Politics

The lack of consolidated will to work for justice in recent decades may be on account of American Christians' diversion of time and effort into political activism that focuses more on the legislating of morality for others than on matters of equality. Political action groups—notably the Moral Majority (1979–late 1980s) and the Christian Coalition (1987–present)—have inadvertently prejudiced people against the simple words of Christ. In their political pursuit of power and outspoken positions on abortion and homosexuality they have given America a picture of Christianity as an angry, intensely judgmental faith. Rather than voicing love for all, the lead personalities in each movement created bully pulpits and blasted opponents with incendiary comments. Non-Christians are highly cynical about a faith that talks about grace, love, and reconciliation and yet cannot express its views without overtones of self-righteousness and hate.

David Kinnaman found that 75 percent of young outsiders, ages sixteen to twenty-nine, felt that Christians were "too involved in politics," while only 41 percent felt that Christianity was "genuine and real." Just 30 percent felt that the faith was "relevant" to their lives.[6]

Tri Robinson also noted:

> Historically the church has struggled with the paradigm of two kingdoms: the kingdom of God and the kingdom of the world. Trying to combine the two is like attempting to mix oil and water. Church history has been consistent on this matter. Every time Christianity has fallen into the trap of using politics to achieve its means, it has lost its power and effectiveness. Relevant Christianity never loses sight of the reality that in the kingdom of God, everything is upside down when contrasted with the world's pursuits. In God's kingdom the greatest is the least; the first is the last; we are to love our enemies; and to be most effective, we are called to servanthood rather than to positions of political power and correctness.[7]

Our faith in Jesus must always be bigger than our political beliefs. In fact, our political leanings should be inconsequential by comparison. Although there may be nothing overtly wrong with rallying for a particular political candidate, we must never believe we are doing so in the name of the Christ. And to use pride, anger, judgment, or inflammatory language when stating our political views is to detract from the reputation of God in our world.

Some Christians even use their Christian faith as the rationale for arguments *against* the protection of human rights for particular individuals. Some Christians have now been associated with the denial of protections for gays and lesbians. It is an ironic and deadly practice for people whose fellow believers are persecuted around the world to do anything but advocate for human rights of all people. We speak out for children, women, minorities, people of other faiths, and all disenfranchised individuals because that is what Jesus did. God is justice; and that justice is especially poignant when it is extended to all people, not just those who follow the tenets of the Christian faith. Which one of us is without sin? Which one of us is not deserving of God's judgment? We are saved only through God's grace, and Christians are called to extend his love.

Jesus spoke public words of protest against the religious leaders and institutions for their lack of integrity and justice, not against unbelievers for their sin. A noted "friend of sinners," Jesus made it clear that his followers were here to love God, help the poor, share the good news, and bless their neighbors.

God derides pious shows, and he is not fooled by acts of fake righteousness.

> Is this the kind of fast I have chosen,
>   only a day for a man to humble himself?
> Is it only for bowing one's head like a reed
>   and for lying on sackcloth and ashes?
> Is that what you call a fast,
>   a day acceptable to the LORD?
>
> Is not this the kind of fasting I have chosen:
> to loose the chains of injustice
>   and untie the cords of the yoke,
> to set the oppressed free
>   and break every yoke?
> Is it not to share your food with the hungry
>   and to provide the poor wanderer with shelter—
> when you see the naked, to clothe him,
>   and not to turn away from your own flesh and blood?
> Then your light will break forth like the dawn,

and your healing will quickly appear;
then your righteousness will go before you,
    and the glory of the LORD will be your rear guard.
Then you will call, and the LORD will answer;
    you will cry for help, and he will say: Here am I.

If you do away with the yoke of oppression,
    with the pointing finger and malicious talk,
and if you spend yourselves in behalf of the hungry
    and satisfy the needs of the oppressed,
then your light will rise in the darkness,
    and your night will become like the noonday.
The LORD will guide you always;
    he will satisfy your needs in a sun-scorched land
    and will strengthen your frame.
You will be like a well-watered garden,
    like a spring whose waters never fail.
Your people will rebuild the ancient ruins
    and will raise up the age-old foundations;
you will be called Repairer of Broken Walls,
    Restorer of Streets with Dwellings. (Isaiah 58:5-12)

As his children, we get to be those repairers of broken walls, the restorers of streets with dwellings.

Blinded by Blame

There are still people who hear of the plight of the poor in our country and are moved to bitterness rather than compassion. They wonder why the poor don't just get a job, pull themselves up by their bootstraps, and stop complaining. They do not see why they should be asked to pay for others' public assistance when they work hard for their money.

There is not an instance in the Bible where Jesus blamed an individual for his or her own troubles. Instead, he talked about his followers' obligation to act when they saw need, demonstrating over and over the amazing transformative power of grace. We are not capable of judging others' deservedness of justice; we are only capable of giving it.

Using a parable, Jesus talked about the judgment that will come when he returns to earth: "When the Son of Man comes in his glory, and all the angels with him, he will sit on his throne in heavenly glory. All the nations will be gathered before him, and he will separate the people one from another as a shepherd separates the sheep from the goats. He will put the sheep on his right and the goats on his left" (Matthew 25:31-33).

The sheep, his righteous, are praised: "For I was hungry and you gave me something to eat, I was thirsty and you gave me something to drink, I was a stranger and you invited me in, I needed clothes and you clothed me, I was sick and you looked after me, I was in prison and you came to visit me" (vv. 35-36).

The righteous do not remember doing this for the king. But he answers, "I tell you the truth, whatever you did for one of the least of these brothers of mine, you did for me" (v. 40).

That is a compelling thought for those of us unsure about our role in this world. The righteous noticed suffering around them and took action. We, too, help the individual and oppose systems of injustice through intervention.

Are the poor deserving of our contempt? Our pity? Are they worth less than those who have achieved the American standard of success? In the Beatitudes, Jesus turned these self-righteous attitudes upside down. He said that "the poor in spirit" are blessed because they will gain "the kingdom of heaven." Those who mourn "will be comforted." The meek "will inherit the earth."

The early Christians were devoted to the implementation of justice for others, perhaps because of the example of the apostles who had walked with Jesus and observed his attitude and actions of justice. Those first followers made sure everyone had enough food. They were even willing to sacrifice their belongings and property to care for others. They served as examples for modern communities of Christians. People of the church must identify the people who are at risk for poverty, systemic racism, abuse, and inadequacies in education—whether children, ethnic minorities, people persecuted because of their beliefs, or individuals ostracized by mainstream society.

True Story

Two friends, a white man and an African American woman, toured a museum exhibit called "Race: Are We So Different?" Anyone who saw them together would have noticed striking differences. He was almost a foot and a half taller than she was. Her hair was thick, beautiful, and black. His head was shaved bald. She was quiet and unassuming. He was outgoing.

The exhibit created by the American Anthropological Association probed topics such as global race mapping; the science of skin; the experience of race in the United States, including housing, land, wealth, health and medicine, and education; and young people. When they came to an exhibit called "Housing and Wealth," they paused in silence. Under a large clear glass box there sat several stacks of money.

Each stack represented, in billions, the per capita amount of money available as earnable income to various racial groups in the United States—Caucasians, Native Americans, African Americans, Hispanics, and so on.

The stack of bills available to white Americans *towered* above the rest. The man suddenly felt his face grow hot. While he stood next to his friend, a single mother who had earned barely enough money to raise her children and still constantly struggled to keep her car in good repair and groceries in her refrigerator, his conscience was on fire. In that moment he knew that his societal system favored him based on the color of his skin. His educational path, vocational training, employment opportunities, and comfortable lifestyle were a demonstration of the disparity between them.

It was more than awkward; it was painful. He had to say something, so he stumbled over these words: "I'm embarrassed, and so sorry. I don't really know what to say to you. I realize that what benefited me cost you, and I don't know what it will take to change this situation. I know it will probably cost me and others something to make this right."

They stood for several seconds in silence. It was only an acknowledgment; but it was a start.

Justice Is Outreach

Our culture is cynical about organized religion, having sometimes been on the receiving end of the church's judgment and aggressive political activism rather than its compassionate practice of faith. Although Christians can be the first ones on the scene of a disaster, generous contributors to people without hope, good neighbors, and outstanding employees, they have not always been known for their swift responses to global issues of injustice. Today the American church is amassing the strength of heart and the resources to speak out in one voice against broader social ills such as poverty, careless treatment of the earth, human trafficking, and homelessness.

From the Bible we know that God is the defender of the poor and the oppressed. Jeremiah 9:23-24 (TNIV) says:

> "Let not the wise boast of their wisdom
>   or the strong boast of their strength
> or the rich boast of their riches,
>   but let those who boast boast about this:
> that they understand and know me,
>   that I am the LORD, who exercises kindness,
> justice and righteousness on earth,
>   for in these I delight," declares the LORD.

Psalm 10:17-18 (TNIV) underscores the point:

> You, LORD, hear the desire of the afflicted;
>   you encourage them, and you listen to their cry,
> defending the fatherless and the oppressed,
>   so that mere earthly mortals
> will never again strike terror.

The justice of God is universal and pertains to all cultures, groups of people, and individuals (see Psalms 76:8-9; 99:1-4; 103:6). God is as concerned about the people of Somalia as he is about the people of South Dakota. He cares equally about Muslims, Hindus, and Christians. He has no less love for those living in poverty than he has for people identified as middle class.

164

God values every person equally, whether an undocumented immigrant or a fifth-generation American citizen. Working side by side with people of all backgrounds, we can serve him by demonstrating that equality and fairness are his design.

Micah: A Profile of Justice

The relentless practice of justice by people of faith is an ancient impulse. The Old Testament prophet Micah, who lived in Judah from 750 B.C. to 686 B.C., devoted himself to addressing inequities between the oppressed and the powerful. His story unfolded in the small town of Moresheth, about twenty-five miles southwest of Jerusalem.

Through bribes and fraud, unscrupulous, elite people were coveting the property and homes of poor people living in small towns and villages. In his writings, Micah made three major accusations against the civic and religious leaders of the nation of Judah. First, he noted that the corrupt government trumped up false charges and illegally confiscated possessions. Second, he pointed out that the priests, prophets, and judges were conspiring in elaborate and fraudulent money-making schemes. Third, Micah accused them of carrying out their schemes with an arrogant sense of religiosity and self-righteousness, as if God had given them permission. He wrote:

> Her leaders judge for a bribe,
> her priests teach for a price,
> and her prophets tell fortunes for money.
> Yet they lean upon the LORD and say,
> "Is not the LORD among us?
> No disaster will come upon us." (Micah 3:11)

In other words, the unjust leaders convinced themselves that no matter how they behaved most of the time, God would defend them because they scrupulously performed religious activities. But humans cannot manipulate God. He transforms *us* when we practice spiritual disciplines with a genuine desire to know him better. As we draw closer to God, he draws closer to us.

So Micah spelled out the projected result of the powerful leaders' continued bad behavior, writing in God's voice:

> I am planning disaster against this people,
>> from which you cannot save yourselves.
> You will no longer walk proudly,
>> for it will be a time of calamity. (Micah 2:3)

Micah imagined these leaders trying to bribe their way out of trouble. Their hubris made even their conversation bloated:

> With what shall I come before the LORD
>> and bow down before the exalted God?
> Shall I come before him with burnt offerings,
>> with calves a year old?
> Will the LORD be pleased with thousands of rams,
>> with ten thousand rivers of oil?
> Shall I offer my firstborn for my transgression,
>> the fruit of my body for the sin of my soul? (Micah 6:6-7)

With stunning and glaring simplicity, Micah provided the antidote to injustice:

> He has showed you, O man, what is good.
>> And what does the LORD require of you?
> To act justly and to love mercy
>> and to walk humbly with your God. (Micah 6:8)

Micah was writing to a specific audience, but his words resonate for the church today. If we were to translate this monologue into twenty-first-century language, it might sound like this: "Shall we add more church services? Should we designate more money to the building fund? Should we increase the number of youth-group events? Really, what religious activities do we need to do to make this right?" Without the heart of God, it is all futile.

So, how do Christians emulate this God of justice? We already listen to the radio, read the news, and have a passing understanding of some of the social justice concerns around the world. But somehow we feel emotionally disconnected— cocooned and safe. How do we move beyond awareness of injustice to involvement? Gathering for worship is invigorating, but worship is designed by God to equip us for action. Studying the Bible is a life-giving discipline, but without personal acts of justice our biblical knowledge remains lifeless, words stuck to pages of paper. Growing deep relationships in community is comforting, but if the community never moves beyond itself to help others, it is functionally blind because it is not seeing and accomplishing the vision of God.

Getting Involved

Wayne Gretzky, the famous Canadian hockey player, said, "You miss 100 percent of the shots you don't take." Taking a shot is where justice begins for Christians. We have to start. Sometimes we just don't know how.

The struggle to connect with the plight of others is not new. The New Testament writer James must have observed it in the early church because he wrote:

What good is it, my brothers and sisters, if people claim to have
faith but have no deeds? Can such faith save them? Suppose a
brother or sister is without clothes and daily food. If one of you
says to them, "Go in peace; keep warm and well fed," but does
nothing about their physical needs, what good is it? In the same
way, faith by itself, if it is not accompanied by action, is dead.
(James 2:14-17 TNIV)

The mind connects with the heart, which connects with the body. We
do something. Guided by the heart of Jesus, ask yourself, "What is
my part in this?" Then ask God to show you where you fit.

Consider these starting points:

- Take action wherever you can in the context in which God has
  placed you. Do not allow injustice to thrive on your block, in
  your workplace, in your school, or within your church.
- Become vulnerable. Avoid defensiveness. Listen to others'
  viewpoints with an open mind and open heart.
- Concern yourself with justice for everybody else—not with
  establishing your own rights.
- Be with people who are facing oppression. When you get to
  know real people, injustice ceases to be impersonal.
- Teach yourself to be outraged by injustice.
- Practice the discipline of prayer intercession on behalf of
  others.
- Think small. Help the church join in local missions trips,
  advocacy groups, neighborhood restoration projects, and
  social mentoring programs—just for starters.
- Think big. Consider how the church can correct social ills on
  a global scale. Work with others—Christians and non-
  Christians—for maximum impact.

Partnering for Good

One of the blessings that the church can bring to its social justice work is partnership.

Churches have always been full of good people working hard to accomplish great things, but sometimes as lone rangers. Churches may find that they are welcome partners in established ministries where they can bring resources, person power, and prayer. Networking with a local food pantry, for instance, helps bring groceries to depleted shelves *and* gives the church a trusted nonprofit resource that is working at the roots of social problems. Once a close relationship is established, the people of the church have the opportunity to refer individuals who come to the door searching for help. This is not to say that churches don't have the joy of creating ministries where none exist. But the duplication of existing organizations will undermine the efforts of good and needy groups. These groups have the experience and the connections already established in the community. They are knowledgeable and dedicated to doing more than just filling the grocery sack. They can help get to the root of social problems in ways the church may not be able to on its own.

Imagine this story of Vanessa, a woman who entered a local church foyer during coffee time and mingled with parishioners. She was middle aged, destitute, and looking for help. Someone brought her cookies and a cup of hot coffee. A man struck up a conversation with her and learned that she was participating in the drug treatment program at the hospital across the street. Vanessa had just been released that morning and had to get some groceries. Could he spare a couple of dollars? He pulled out his wallet and found a twenty-dollar bill, which she took gladly, thanking him. As she moved away he said he would pray for her.

The following week Vanessa returned for coffee, cookies, and conversation. People she hadn't met the week before asked her name and learned her story. She was in desperate need of transportation to and from her apartment. One couple only had a five-dollar bill but gave it to her. She moved to a visitor at the church who was sipping coffee by herself. Vanessa told her story and the young woman, embarrassed, gave her a couple of dollars. With seven dollars in her purse Vanessa sat down in one of the foyer chairs and fell asleep. One of the pastors had to wake her gently when the building was being closed.

At the Monday morning meeting pastors and staff all had stories of people Vanessa had approached the day before. There was a mixture of tenderness and embarrassment among those individuals. They wanted to help, but they were beginning to feel embarrassed by the pattern of the requests for cash. Vanessa had angrily refused someone's offer to call her social worker. They were beginning to feel that people would not be able to meet all of Vanessa's needs week after week.

Hearing the story, one staff member exclaimed, "I know Vanessa. She used to come here last year." She had approached people for money then, too. But receiving donations did not fill the void.

Everyone was frustrated—the givers who could not do enough, the visitors to the church who were put on the spot when asked for money, and the staff who felt unsure of the proper response in the face of obvious need.

A week later a team of leaders and volunteers toured the local food pantry that they were hoping to partner with in the community. During a talk describing the many resources they offered to people in the neighborhood, the director of the program said, "We advise people not to give cash. Instead, direct people here. We meet with every person who comes to this agency, get to know them, pray with them, and keep good records. We can help with job searches, housing, and connections with other resources."

The volunteers looked at one another. Was this a giant opt-out on their part? Hadn't Jesus said, "Feed the hungry"?

The program director understood their concern but explained that what the agency could really use was a strong partnership— a willingness for volunteers to come and work one-on-one with the people at the food pantry and for the food pantry to involve the church community in their more strategic and integrated efforts to help struggling people like Vanessa.

Before recreating a ministry that already exists in your city, investigate local resources. Is there a group in your area that could use a partner in ministry? Go for a tour. Find out how your church can join in a committed and dedicated way. Do not impose your methodology; look to see how you can be used and how you can grow in a relationship and dedicate yourselves to working together for an extended period of time.

Transforming the Church

God hates injustice. Our faith communities must lead the way in organizing people for greater effectiveness. Our awareness must increase, but so must our action. God's demand for justice is so central to Christianity that all the other responses we could give to God are empty or diminished without it. But when we work toward social justice our invisible faith in God becomes instantly visible and real. We should not be overly concerned about what others think, but the Christian's emphasis on justice will have a tremendous effect. Justice demonstrates real faith to a culture that is highly cynical of people who talk about grace, love, and reconciliation and yet do little to demonstrate them. Some Christians have even worked against expressions of justice such as immigration reform and assistance to the poor. Justice can turn that tide around. Regardless of political views on controversial topics, the church can passionately express that Jesus cares about all people, and his followers do, too.

As Christians we can talk endlessly about what we believe, but our actions must speak louder than words. The Apostle Paul wrote to the church in Corinth: "We are therefore Christ's ambassadors, as though God were making his appeal through us" (2 Corinthians 5:20). The presence of Jesus Christ in us becomes the presence of Jesus Christ in the world.

Heavenly Father, clarify the issues of social injustice that are both far away and near to us. Teach us to love mercy as you do. Give us compassion and direction to know how to give more mercy to others, then empower us and direct us to walk with others and see their plights. Give us the resources and desire to intervene. We want to be like you and transform the world through our actions and your power. We pray in Jesus' name. Amen.

Start Translating

1. Guide your congregation through these personal reflection questions:

Where do you see concerns of social justice around you? Who are the victims of injustice?

Why has social justice not been as important of a focus for many churches as other issues?

What are two or three actions you can take in the area of social justice that will demonstrate God's love for others?

Who is a non-Christian friend or acquaintance with whom you can partner on a social justice project?

2. Get a sense of God's concern for justice in his world. Look up the word *justice* in a Bible concordance (online Bibles like www.biblegateway.com or www.biblica.com have free searchable concordances) and read the listed verses. Write down your favorites and consider how God's love of justice affects your own sense of what is just and fair for others.

3. Do research on justice matters on a global scale and ask God to help your church with filling a need. Incorporate this social justice issue into your worship service and make it a special focus of prayer for a year.

4. Read Nehemiah 5:1-13 and have a discussion about the potential for your congregation to have internal justice struggles. Where are your prejudices? Acknowledge racism. Look at the model of Nehemiah.

5. Invite speakers to talk to your congregation about justice issues in your community (for instance, inequalities in education, housing, or resource accessibility; racism or immigration issues). Spend time afterward talking about how

these issues intersect with the Bible, Jesus' teachings, and the Christian life. How will your community address these issues?

6. Form small reading groups. Together, read *Everyday Justice: The Global Impact of Our Daily Choices* by Julie Clawson, or *Social Justice Handbook: Small Steps for a Better World* by Mae Elise Cannon.

7. Research ministries located in your area. Tour their operations. Get to know them. Select one or two that will become local partners in social justice. Involve your community through regular and concentrated volunteer opportunities.

8. Invite students in your church to participate in outreach projects that address justice in our world.

CHAPTER NINE

CULTURALLY ENGAGED

Building Bridges of Identification

May God be gracious to us and bless us
and make his face shine upon us,
that your ways may be known on earth,
your salvation among all nations. (Psalm 67:1-2)

What is culture and what does it have to do with the church? Some Christians, equating the notion of culture with only negative associations, say that church and culture are two separate worlds, polar opposites that should not overlap. The reality is that culture and church are inextricably linked, and how they relate to each other has much to do with how accessible faith is to people outside the church. Some Christians have tried to hold mainstream culture, labeled "secular," at a distance. Notably since the cataclysmic societal changes of the 1960s, some Christians feel angry, suspicious, or uncomfortable. This isolation has not been helpful to the church. Whereas Christians are called to live like Jesus ("Whatever is true, whatever is noble, whatever is right, whatever is pure, whatever is lovely, whatever is admirable—if anything is excellent or praiseworthy—think about such things," Philippians 4:8), they are not called to avoid engagement with people unlike them. When the church withdraws from culture, it creates a nearly insurmountable barrier to the message of Jesus. To continue to do so into the future would be devastating to the cause of the Christ.

What is culture, anyway? One prominent Christian organization defines it this way: "In the broadest sense . . . [culture is] simply the patterned way in which people do things together."[1] There are innumerable subsets within culture. Even churches have cultures. The American church is called to minister inside American culture and also within the global culture.

Christian Mission and Popular Culture

A crisis of mission occurs when churches do not discipline themselves to move out of their own culture to build bridges to the surrounding culture. It is obvious when a church has not begun to have this conversation. The people inside are not aware of their idiosyncrasies or the reality of the rapidly changing world around them. The effect is that people bed down in their church subcultures and fall into a Rip Van Winkle slumber. This is why walking into some churches is like stepping into a time warp. Anyone outside that culture who enters, whether out of curiosity or accident, is likely to feel dramatically out of place and uncomfortable.

Bent on self-preservation, some churches become buttressed and retrenched behind walls of separation. Church leaders can know if this is happening by honestly answering these questions: "Are we spending more time sustaining our doctrines, systems, and programs than engaging the people and culture around us?" "Do we expect people to come to us rather than us going to them in service?" and "If we were to level our church building and leave the area, would the community miss us? Would they even know we were gone?" Although sustaining Bible studies and events are vital and valuable work, they are not enough. When a church is not blessing and engaging the people of its community, it is not meeting its fullest potential or its God-given mission.

Jesus Demonstrated Cultural Engagement

The self-preservation of church subcultures is neither biblical nor the pattern of Jesus as he lived out God's mission. There can be little doubt that Jesus knew popular culture well. He shared stories that embraced everyday reality. He taught where people gathered, not just in religious buildings. He was aware of the local scene. At one point Jesus called King Herod a fox (Luke 13:32), intimating his knowledge of the power games that Herod played between the Roman government and the local Jewish authorities.

The most striking feature of Jesus' interaction with popular culture was that he never attacked it (Greek culture, art, games, or theater). Rather than being oppositional to popular culture, he deconstructed the "church" culture of his day, building bridges through relationships.

Some churches have argued against involvement in culture, but the importance of building bridges now must become a non-negotiable commitment. When people from the broader culture interact with Christians or visit places of worship and experience dramatic cultural irrelevance, they will not be back. They will be not only uninterested but distanced. Today people no longer feel obligated to participate in church, a shift that began with baby boomers leaving the church upon reaching adulthood in the 1960s and 1970s. Prior to this period many generations of Western churches enjoyed the benefit of cultural affinity, but the notion that church attendance is obligatory or even status quo has now been thoroughly disassembled. This creates an urgent need for the church to adjust its cultural assumptions and behavior.

While some evangelicals embraced the opportunity to engage culture after this fracture, mainline churches and some evangelicals opposed what they viewed as "watering down the gospel," a concern more rooted in personal taste than in actual danger. A percentage never made the cultural shift. They stayed the course and assumed that people would come as they always had. They didn't. Although the support of older members has kept these churches alive, they have not experienced an influx of new believers who can passionately take the faith community into the next century.

Steeping ourselves in our own safe and familiar church culture can inure us to this reality. Numbers presented by polling groups sometimes claim that more than 40 percent of Americans attend church; but David T. Olson, author of *The American Church in Crisis*, writes: "If Christians were to look around, they would find that far fewer Americans are following their lead and authentically connecting to a local church than they might think."[2] He goes on to say:

> Most Christians have not noticed the silent decay of the American church. Instead, we hear the success stories of Willow Creek, The Potter's House, Saddleback, and Rob Bell's Mars Hill; we discover that more than 30 million people have

read *The Purpose-Driven Life*; and we believe the results of opinion polls that show thriving church attendance. Beneath this veneer of success, however, lies a church in decline.[3]

It is time for the church to see reality. We *must* engage. We must stop cutting and pasting grids for superficial success and get into the deeper water of holistic faith. It will require building genuine and caring relationships with people outside of our church communities and cultures. This is true for all churches: those that are just now realizing the value of living within culture as Jesus did, those that need to expand their grid from twentieth-century corporate church models to one that speaks to the genuine needs of people searching for spiritual answers today, and those new church starts and redevelopments that are completely redesigned and reenergized.

The See-through Church

The work of creating bridges to the surrounding culture begins by establishing a high level of transparency between the gathered church and its context. Creating and maintaining transparency between a faith community and the surrounding community is an arduous and ongoing task. Robert Lewis, author of *The Church of Irresistible Influence*, contends that churches fail to maintain bridges to their surrounding culture because of three factors:

1. The larger a church grows, the more it tends to be most concerned with itself.

2. The church has an inability to maintain a balance of public proclamation and congregational presence and action in the context.
3. The church fails to overcome obstacles to making bridges to culture. These obstacles include fear, confusion, lack of direction, and confusion over what is considered "success."[4]

To create bridges and remain transparent as a visible community of faith, churches must assess what is being said and communicated every week. They must evaluate their corporate worship and messaging against the three factors that Lewis describes. Furthermore, leaders must have the courage to identify whether their congregational members are doing the work of mission beyond the walls of the church building.

Christian Mission and Global Culture

The church also faces the challenge of the larger reality of global culture around it. American Christianity must prepare to welcome and embrace the coming wave of multiculturalism. Although the American church reflects many ethnic cultures, it has, until now, remained largely segregated. The future holds a different scenario because the largest growth of the church will come through ethnic streams. In a few decades, the whole American church will be a mosaic. If we want to prepare to be in that movement and thrive, we must make changes now.

For a biblical example of our current crossroad, we look to Jonah, who confronted a new reality and demonstrated resistance to following God across global culture. Although the story of Jonah has typically been told as one man's temporary disobedience and restoration, we also need to see how his story mirrors the struggle going on in the contemporary church. The Israelite culture of the day was inherently monocultural, but God asked Jonah to move beyond his cultural myopia. From Jonah's experience we learn that we must show the compassion of God to *all* people, even if it throws us out of our comfort zone.

However, speak the words "diverse church" and many Christian leaders look disoriented. This is a new—and overwhelming—challenge. Church leaders know that when creating brochures and websites it is important to show photographs (or stock photographs) of people of color so that our congregations look diverse. But many Christian institutions and organizations cannot truly claim to be racially diverse. Even with earnest desire, we do not know how to begin. Or we convince ourselves that the community around the church is not racially diverse, and therefore our congregation is exempt. Or we have not opened ourselves to admitting our past failings in issues of race. Overall, the church has not been willing to exert the effort and resources to correct the imbalance.

But we must recognize that America is becoming diverse and the world is more globally connected. The technology and communication revolution has radically changed how connected we are to one another. Consider:

- Twenty years ago there were maybe four hundred people on the planet who understood the power of the World Wide Web and today there are approximately 1.7 billion.[5]
- Twenty years ago there were 11.1 million cell phone users in the world.[6] (That is a slightly smaller amount of people than the Los Angeles metro population.) At the end of 2009 an

estimated 4.6 billion people around the globe had cellular access.[7] That is nearly two-thirds of the world's population.

* A recent survey of American college students showed that some college students will only read on average eight books a year but 2,300 webpages![8]

In the connectivity of communication and the rapidly changing immigration patterns of American culture we see the inevitability of global culture becoming increasingly synonymous with local culture. Soong-Chan Rah, a professor at North Park Theological Seminary in Chicago and author of *The Next Evangelicalism: Freeing the Church from Western Cultural Captivity*, notes:

> The unavoidable reality is that, by the year 2050, projections point to a nation without an ethnic majority. America will no longer be a Eurocentric, white nation. Furthermore . . . the non-white population among Christians is growing at a rate faster than the general population. American Christianity will become nonwhite before the rest of American society. Even now, most denominations are faced with the reality that unless they see growth among the ethnic minority population within their denomination, they will experience steady decline.[9]

Churches can choose to have the critical conversation about living in a multicultural world now or be forced to do so in twenty-five to forty years. If we are to have a credible faith, we must ask a very serious question: How are we preparing the church of Jesus to move into the globally connected and intercultural age?

Our New World and Worldview

If we are to effectively translate our faith to the people around us, as American Christians we must change how we think about people from cultures different from our own. It means we welcome people of all global backgrounds, those who previously would have been considered strangers.

The United States is considered the most multicultural country in the world. As of 2006, the United States accepted more immigrants as permanent residents than any other country in the world.[10] Some believe that soon the immigrant portion of the U.S. population will exceed 14.8 percent. Many congregations founded in the late nineteenth and early twentieth centuries experienced major growth and vitality as they boldly served and reached out to immigrants. The nationalities may have changed, but the reality is the same.

Yet, there is a continual struggle in the process of nurturing diversity in the church. Prejudice and misinformation remain serious problems. It seems that cultural and ethnic bias can be one of the last things touched by the spiritual process of sanctification as God regenerates our thinking and values. We must move past our personal and institutionalized prejudices.

Broad cultural stereotyping continues to be a rampant problem in America, but the church can begin to challenge itself to confront and change that reality. God makes no distinction between American, Mexican, Iraqi, Russian, Turk, Japanese, Australian, Egyptian, or Israeli. If that thought makes us feel defensive, sad, or uncomfortable, we must like Jonah realign our viewpoint and ideals with God's.

In the book of Revelation, we get a slim glimpse of eternity through a vision John received. Standing in the eternal presence of God was a great multitude that no one could count, with individuals from every nation, tribe, people, and language (7:9). We must long for that kind of cultural perspective, moving beyond our self-centered cultural pride to God's vision. Should we appreciate America and value its system of governance? Yes. Such an attitude is part of good citizenship. Should we love people of all countries and cultures as ourselves? Yes. This is part of an even more important eternal citizenship.

A Biblical Directive on Diversity

God made it clear to the early disciples that the message of Jesus was for everyone and that the disciples must reach out beyond their comfortable circles. Peter received this directive in an unforgettable manner. Acts 10 tells the story of Cornelius, a centurion living in Caesarea, who commanded a large number of soldiers in the Roman army. One day he experienced a vision of an angel telling him to send men to Joppa to find a man named Peter who was staying with Simon the tanner. Cornelius did as he was instructed. The next day, two of his servants were approaching Joppa about the same time Peter went to the roof to pray. Peter saw a vision of heaven opening. A large sheet was lowered to earth by its corners, and on it were all kinds of animals, birds, and reptiles. A voice said, "Go on, Peter. You're hungry. Kill and eat." The godly Jewish man protested, "I have never eaten anything impure or unclean in my life," but the voice answered, "Do not call anything impure that God has made clean!" This happened three times. Then the sheet was taken back to heaven.

At this moment the servants of Cornelius arrived at Simon's house and stopped at the gate. The Holy Spirit said to Peter, "Don't hesitate to go with them, because they were sent by me." Peter obeyed but he was surprised to see that they were obviously Gentiles, not Jews. Perhaps his first instinct was to draw back, but he went out to meet them and said, "I am the one you're looking for." The visitors explained their mission and Peter invited them inside as his guests.

The next day Peter and some of the Jesus followers from Joppa journeyed with the men to Caesarea. Cornelius was waiting expectantly with a large welcoming group of friends and family. Peter stood among the people, very conscious that it was against Hebrew law for a Jew to associate with Gentiles. Peter could have refused to enter. He could have followed God in all areas but this one. He could have changed history by keeping the law he had been taught since boyhood. Instead, Peter got the message: God did not show favoritism.

God gave Peter a dramatic vision that expanded his cultural worldview—an important step in the extension of Christianity to people of all cultural backgrounds. It is unlikely that Peter or any of the disciples would have thought of this idea themselves. There was a strong culture of separatism among the Jewish people at that time. God had set them apart as his holy people.

But God had both a plan and perfect timing. There were signs pointing to this change, and when it finally happened—when God made it clear that non-Jewish people would be welcomed into the kingdom of God—there were birthing pains. Jesus' followers struggled with this new expectation that they must welcome *all* people into their community of belief.

We tend to read this account and think of it as a one-time event that has little impact on our thinking or behavior today. "It happened to Peter, everything changed, and here we are." But God is still drawing people to him. He asks for our active involvement in making the way of Jesus open to everyone.

Grappling with Discomfort

In Acts 10:34-35, Peter said: "I now realize how true it is that God does not show favoritism, but accepts those who fear him and do what is right" (TNIV). He then went on to teach and discuss Jesus with several non-Jewish people, and it all led to many people becoming followers of Christ. This was worthy of celebration! Caught up in the excitement of the moment, Peter may have been unprepared for what followed: "The apostles and the believers throughout Judea heard that the Gentiles also had received the word of God. So when Peter went up to Jerusalem, the circumcised believers criticized him and said, 'You went into the house of the uncircumcised and ate with them'" (Acts 11:1-3 TNIV). Other Christians challenged and criticized him. How disheartening.

After he explained exactly what happened, however, and painted the perspective of the Gentiles, the Christians throughout the region also began to understand. The biblical account notes: "When they heard this, they had no further objections and praised God, saying, 'So then, even to Gentiles God has granted repentance that leads to life'" (Acts 11:18 TNIV). Sometimes all we need is perspective and background to help us grapple with what is at first new and uncomfortable.

God clearly told Peter that the doors were wide open for all to enter. We know that the same is true for us. We are called to welcome people who are estranged from their homes and countries. But first we need to understand the circumstances and lives of refugees and immigrants. In an interview about the lifestyles of refugees and immigrants in America, Damon Schroeder, a director of World Relief (a Christian international relief and development agency), spoke of the challenges that people uprooted from their homes face.[11] He painted a bleak picture. The loneliness and isolation are intense. Immigrants and refugees have left their communities, families, and the familiarity of home, customs, dress, weather, food, sounds, and sights. They may not speak the language, have transportation, or understand what is needed to survive in their new location. All of this strangeness can accentuate other issues they are facing—poverty, depression, and culture shock.

There are intergenerational issues. Sometimes the children are the ones who have picked up the new language and must translate for their parents. Because of this transposing of responsibility, the children sometimes are forced to make family decisions, which can be disempowering to parents. There is tension over the desire of parents to shield their children from the vices of American youth culture and to preserve traditions of the old environment. This can create tremendous rifts in the family.

We need to know that many refugee families have experienced trauma—terrible poverty, imprisonment, crime, or torture. They may have seen family members killed in front of them. They may be suffering from the aftereffects of war or persecution. All of these factors can contribute to them being at risk for substance abuse, domestic violence, poverty, homelessness, job loss, and family dissolution.

Overcoming the Sin of Prejudice

One of the greatest challenges of the early church was giving up cultural prejudice. Only a dramatic message from God could shake loose Peter's biases about who was in and who was out. God challenged Peter to do something more significant than change his eating habits. He was called to recognize that the Jewish culture of his day was merely *one* culture in a *world* of cultures that Jesus came to save. Peter was challenged to repent and admit the error of his bigotry, make a change in attitude, and put his new perspective into practice. The story suggests that even mature Christians need periodic paradigm shifts in order to come into line with God's thinking.

How do modern Christians repent of the sins of bigotry and bias? It will be a long process, but we must first recognize and confess the sin.

How, then, does the church begin to embrace diversity and minister to the diverse people God has brought into our communities? One answer may be offered by Soong-Chan Rah, who notes that the church can readily access the insight, guidance, and perspective of leaders and laypeople of color.

> The Western, white captivity of the church can be overcome by the humble willingness to submit to the spiritual authority of nonwhites. Will white evangelicals who have never been in a position of submission to nonwhites see this situation as an unacceptable state? Are white evangelicals willing to enter into places of submission (maybe for the first time in their lives) to those outside of their ethnic group?[12]

We must learn and listen. We must spend time with our neighbors and deliberately and specifically seek their participation and leadership in our churches. We must have a new picture of God's beautiful vision for the church when he sent his Son.

Start with prayer. Pray that Christians will be willing to join in cross-cultural work that extends the mercy, love, and helping hands of Jesus to strangers in our midst. Be faithful in prayer. Ask for God's help as you open yourself up to cultural engagement. Seek his perspective and wisdom.

True Story

Thomas, the pastor of a downtown congregation, typically drove in from the suburbs each morning and out in the late afternoon, his feet never moving farther than a couple of blocks beyond the office. One afternoon he walked. He walked beyond the parameters of his church. He walked past the headquarters of large and powerful companies; condemned houses situated next to upscale lofts; people of all colors, nationalities, and backgrounds; restaurants serving fragrant and unfamiliar ethnic foods; and run-down, turn-of-the-century homes and high-rise retirement communities where people of various economic situations came and went. There were fast-food joints, five-star restaurants, commercial buildings, gospel missions, parking ramps, and empty lots. His fluctuating emotions gave him whiplash. He was troubled by a clear sense of his personal prejudices. With each step, glance, and smell he grappled with a mix of discomfort, uneasiness, and an expanded viewpoint.

Back inside the church, he looked at his surroundings with new eyes. The walk had, in a small way, forced him to interact with the reality of the world. It would not be enough to merely create worship services and post a "Welcome" greeting on the church marquee. Inviting people of diverse backgrounds into the church—individuals of different nationalities, backgrounds, and socioeconomic groups—would require true outreach and service. He needed God to help reconstruct his beliefs, opinions, and judgments toward people and places.

Extending Hospitality

By inviting them into his home, Peter extended hospitality to the people that Cornelius sent. Likewise, Cornelius extended hospitality to Peter. We should not underestimate the level of personal commitment it took to respond with hospitality. We are given the same opportunities, and it is often difficult to respond with the required level of openness and warmth. Yet this is the depth of the Christian hospitality we seek. This is where cultural engagement becomes real.

The eternal value of showing love to strangers is demonstrated in a mystical story about Abraham and his wife Sarah. In Genesis, three men wanted to meet with Abraham. They approached him while he was sitting at the entrance of his tent. Sensing something special about these visitors, Abraham hurried from his tent, "bowed low to the ground," and said, "If I have found favor in your eyes . . . do not pass your servant by. Let a little water be brought, and then you may all wash your feet and rest under this tree. Let me get you something to eat, so you can be refreshed and then go on your way" (Genesis 18:2-5).

The three men were representatives of God. Abraham and his wife Sarah extended hospitality to these strangers at personal risk and inconvenience. They did not understand, at first, that they were extending hospitality to God. This is exactly what Jesus taught in the parable of the sheep and the goats, reminding his followers—and us—that whatever we do for the stranger we do for him (see Matthew 25:40).

Breaking Down Our Barriers

There is a reason we do not attend to the presence of Jesus in the lives of strangers. It is not for lack of opportunity. Steering away from engagement with others is a result of apathy, over-scheduling, and even hostility.

Apathy is the by-product of misinformation. We are misinformed about our place and purpose on earth; we do not understand or identify with people of different cultures; we intentionally remain cold to their needs and concerns. We just don't care.

Overscheduling in our culture is rampant. Our careers require long hours and intense focus. Our children's schedules are as busy as our own. We already have more social obligations than we know how to keep and our calendar of responsibilities squeezes out any possibility of interaction with people in cultures other than our own. We are so committed that we can rarely spare an evening or a weekend to assist people in need. We would *like* to spend time pursuing richer interactions with people of different backgrounds, but the kids have soccer practice, piano lessons, and youth group.

Hostility is also the result of misinformation and sin. We view people of other cultures as enemies to be mistrusted. We don't like the way they infringe on our way of doing things—what language is spoken, what foods are served, and what programs are available in our schools. We worry and discuss our own preferences and neglect the stranger in our midst.

The Only Response

These obstacles to cultural engagement may seem insurmountable. Yet, there was a moment when a religious leader asked Jesus, "Of all the commandments, which is the most important?" Jesus replied: " 'You must love the Lord your God with all your heart, all your soul, all your mind, and all your strength.' The second is equally important: 'Love your neighbor as yourself.' No other commandment is greater than these" (Mark 12:28, 30-31 NLT).

Loving and interacting in a meaningful way with others is our way of opening ourselves to Jesus. His instructions were clear, and our response must be unmistakably loving. When we do this we will be culturally engaged with our fellow human beings and fully engaged with God.

Great God of all people, we confess our sins of apathy, busyness, and hostility toward people you love. Open our eyes to the needs around us. Give us humility and understanding as we struggle with feelings that are uncomfortable. As we learn to accept differences, give us the time and desire to pause in our hectic lives. Let us know how to pray for people of other cultures. Give us the courage to repent of our prejudices. Teach us the practice of hospitality. We do these things as we would do them for your Son, praying in the name of Jesus. Amen.

Start Translating

1. Guide your congregation through these personal reflection questions:

   How would you define popular culture? What biases do you have toward the culture around you? Are they warranted?

   What do you know about the global culture in your neighborhood? Are you isolated from this culture? What cultures are present within a twenty-mile radius of your church and home?

   How—and how often—do you interact with these groups of people?

   What are the needs of the people of other cultures that surround you?

   How is your church involved in the lives of people from other cultures? How can it be more involved?

2. Invite leaders and members of your congregation to take a walking tour of businesses, housing units, entertainment venues, parks, restaurants, and so forth in your neighborhood. Walk back into your building. What comparisons do

you see? How would a newcomer see your space? Your communications? Your worship experience?

3. Ask people in your church to pretend it is their first time in the building. Provide two pads of different colored sticky notes. Ask them to label areas and items in the church as "culturally relevant" or "irrelevant." Label everything from light switches to carpeting. What things are impediments? This exercise should not be about improving the look of the church but about making it accessible to the culture in which you serve.

4. Ask an outsider or group of outsiders to enter the church and talk about their first impressions and comfort level.

5. See a movie with a group of church leaders. Spend time over coffee talking about assumptions inherent in the film. Are they reflective of society at large? How does your church address or relate to those assumptions?

6. Commit yourself to learning about and working toward racial reconciliation. Research, attend seminars, or read books that will expand your understanding of the issue of global culture and racial reconciliation. Partner with agencies in your community that are working toward the goal of bringing about partnerships between communities.

7. Commit to praying for people who are strangers in your community. Ask that God help the church become more culturally aware and sensitive to issues of race.

CHAPTER TEN

GRACE-FILLED

Reflecting the Lavish Love of God

But because of his great love for us, God, who is rich in mercy, made us alive with Christ even when we were dead in transgressions. . . . For it is by grace you have been saved, through faith — and this not from yourselves, it is the gift of God—not by works, so that no one can boast. For we are God's workmanship, created in Christ Jesus to do good works, which God prepared in advance for us to do. (Ephesians 2:4, 8-10)

For many people, grace is a commodity rarely encountered. As civility falls out of fashion in our rushed culture, we are more likely to experience disinterest, rudeness, and even rage from the people around us. In litigious America, kindness can often be displaced by suspicion and the golden rule exchanged for "an eye for an eye."

In this harsh terrain the church has the glorious opportunity to be the consistent source of hope and relief that God intended. Through his community of believers, God shares the grace of Jesus, meeting people where they are and extending his unexpected, undeserved gift of transformation and salvation.

Christians in our culture are called to mirror his generosity by offering grace with abandon.

The Church's Choice

Whether justified in their belief or not, many individuals now feel that the church is the last place they will find grace. Bitter experiences with misguided, self-righteous individuals and institutions have convinced them that within mainstream evangelical communities they will be judged and condemned rather than accepted and loved. Repelled by the exclusive-club mentality that they have seen and experienced there, some have resolved to steer clear of church even though they believe in God. Others have gone further, rejecting belief altogether.

Yet the world aches for grace.

As the appeal of Christianity shrinks in America, the Christian church is at a crossroads. Will it offer grace only to people who dress, act, and think in prescribed ways, or will it be as lavish as God in sharing the news of Jesus' transformative power? In order for Christianity to make sense in our context, we must give grace away freely, blind to everything but the recipient's desire for the gift.

The Historical Roots of Grace

The Bible is rich with grace. The Old Testament uses the Hebrew word *chen*, meaning "favor." The New Testament writers referred to the grace of God by using the Greek word *charis*, understood as "unmerited favor."

In the book of Acts, Luke, a brilliant physician and eyewitness to the work of the apostles, recorded the important events of the Christian church during its first years of existence—shocking, supernatural encounters with God. When the Christian church was officially born fifty days after Jesus' resurrection, there were only about 120 followers on earth. This meager group had gathered for prayer on Pentecost, the Jewish festival day. God sent his Holy Spirit to empower them, and in a matter of minutes the church grew to 3,120.

Twenty years later, thousands of Christians were participating in small and large churches scattered through the ancient Roman Empire. What started as a movement exclusive to the Jewish faith spread to people of diverse cultural backgrounds, which naturally created some organizational and theological difficulties. One matter of contention was whether non-Jewish Christians (known as "Gentile Christians") needed to adhere to the Jewish customs and regulations. Grace intersected with faith in the adoption of new people to Christianity.

Key leaders of the early church called a meeting in Jerusalem to discuss what had become a problem large enough to threaten the health and stability of the entire Christian church. In what is now known as the Council of Jerusalem, the apostle Peter stood up after a lot of discussion on both sides of the argument and said:

> Brothers, you know that some time ago God made a choice among you that the Gentiles might hear from my lips the message of the gospel and believe. God, who knows the heart, showed that he accepted them by giving the Holy Spirit to them, just as he did to us. He did not discriminate between us and them, for he purified their hearts by faith. Now then, why do you try to test God by putting on the necks of Gentiles a

yoke that neither we nor our ancestors have been able to bear?
No! We believe it is through the grace of our Lord Jesus that we
are saved, just as they are. (Acts 15:7-11 TNIV)

This speech by Peter, the preeminent pastor to Jewish
Christians in Jerusalem, is considered a watershed moment for the
church. Peter summarizes the faith beautifully, saying that God
makes no distinction between any believers, cleanses them
through faith alone, and saves people through the undeserved
grace of Jesus. Nothing can stand in the way of sincere people
asking to receive grace. Our favorite church traditions, assumptions, and practices must continually be scrutinized to see if they
trip people up or cloud or distort the transmission of grace
through faith alone.

The Jerusalem Council agreed with Peter's wisdom, and the
major theological dispute was resolved. The decision set the tone
for how Christians are to relate to one another and to new people
coming to faith. Whether we have been faithful followers of Jesus
for fifty years, new believers for five minutes, or remain skeptics,
we all stand on common ground: in need of the undeserved grace
of Jesus Christ.

Historic biblical theology recognizes that God gives to us two
forms of grace. "Common grace" is what God gives to all of creation, providing for its continuing existence. Jesus said: "[God]
gives his sunlight to both the evil and the good, and he sends rain
on the just and the unjust alike" (Matthew 5:45b NLT). That's
common grace.

"Special grace" is the grace by which God specifically forgives
our sin and helps us become whole people. It is God-initiated and
not human invented. It is not based upon merit. It works. And it is

sufficient. It is completely adequate to solve our problem of separation from God.

Needing Grace

We always begin by recognizing our need for grace. Each of us is imperfect and unable to solve our own need for restoration with God. Too proud, too distracted, too weak, we all come to God with a sinful nature that is impossible to alleviate by ourselves. We must recognize the need for grace in every aspect of Christian community. God invites us to receive forgiveness and salvation through faith in Jesus.

God pursues us relentlessly with his grace. We may be proud, busy, apathetic, or doubtful. We may be racing away from God, too caught up in the pursuit of success, pleasure, and responsibilities to turn and accept his offer. We may feel too weak and unworthy to even look to God for help. It is harder to recognize our need for grace than we like to admit.

The Apostle Paul in the New Testament knew just how hard it was. At the time of his conversion he was a sadistic persecutor of followers of "the Way." But Jesus appeared to Paul with an unearthly brilliance that was, literally, blinding. Paul fell to the ground and was without sight for three days. Eventually God's grace overwhelmed Paul, and he became an unlikely follower of Jesus.

Several years later he taught the topic of grace to a church in Ephesus (located in modern-day Turkey). Paul wrote:

> As for you, you were dead in your transgressions and sins, in which you used to live when you followed the ways of this

world and of the ruler of the kingdom of the air, the spirit who
is now at work in those who are disobedient. All of us also lived
among them at one time, gratifying the cravings of our sinful
nature and following its desires and thoughts. Like the rest, we
were by nature objects of wrath. (Ephesians 2:1-3)

God presents his rich grace to us on the proverbial silver platter.

Receiving Grace

Recognizing our need for grace is only our first step. We must
actually receive it. One way to understand this "receiving"
process is to think of going through a door—a portal to a new
reality. It is a new world of grace. The rules that previously guided
life no longer apply. Forgiveness, freedom, and peace are the gifts
given to everyone who passes through this door. Paul taught that
saving grace is a gift and not something that you earn. He taught:
"If you confess with your mouth, 'Jesus is Lord,' and believe in
your heart that God raised him from the dead, you will be saved.
For it is with your heart that you believe and are justified, and it
is with your mouth that you confess and are saved" (Romans
10:9-10). These are not magic words; they are words that signify
an inner decision and a change in direction. Making the decision
to receive grace is the most important decision we can make
because it brings us into relationship and reconciliation with God.

Receiving grace does not stop with the words "I believe." We
are in a constant state of grace, growing to become more like
Jesus every day. When he said, "Go and sin no more" to the
woman caught in adultery, he was not just giving her a directive
to stop her behavior. He was telling her to seek ongoing whole-
ness in God. If the only thing that happened in the Samaritan

woman's life was the ceasing of her promiscuous behavior, it would have been a very small outcome for an encounter with the Messiah. We are like that woman, always humble before God—forgiven but never forgetting our ongoing sinfullness and his grace to us.

Giving Grace

Once we have received grace it is necessary that we also give it—individually as Christians and corporately as the church.

It is ironic that some believers can become so conceited or self-righteous that they begrudge grace to others or judge people who have not experienced faith in the Christ. Feeling above temptation, we allow ourselves to feel scandalized or offended by the behavior of non-Christians. We would go so far as to deny grace to them until they meet our standards for righteousness. Having forgotten our humble beginnings, we become unwilling to convey grace to others, creating a hierarchy of sins. Our sins are near the bottom of the list. Others' are near the top. We do not see how God could provide grace without these people first cleaning up their lives to our satisfaction.

But the Bible is unequivocal: the law does not save anyone. Our own attempts to be holy are doomed to fail. We try—and with the power of the Holy Spirit we sometimes overcome. But there has never been an individual who could become sin-free by deciding to live a different life or by becoming a Christian. Knowing this should fill us with humility. Knowing this should keep us from ever looking at another individual's sin as disgusting, unforgivable, or an impediment to grace. Only God can convey grace, and he does it with abandon for the people we view as the most unworthy.

Time and again, God sought the people others would have shunned. Jesus was consistent. His conversations began with grace. People didn't have to work their way there. He saw the greedy tax collector (perhaps our equivalent of a modern-day scam artist or exploitive corporate executive) and said, "I want to have dinner with you tonight." We, likewise, are called to show understanding to the people in our path—not to identify their sins and condemn them.

How do we maintain the humility we need to resist judging others? We become sensitive to the ways we fail God and others every day. We recognize that we were not naturally born into the kingdom of God but have been adopted. John, one of the biographers of Jesus, wrote: "To all who received [Jesus Christ], to those who believed in his name, he gave the right to become children of God—children born not of natural descent, nor of human decision . . . but born of God" (John 1:12-13). We are like adopted children.

There was a family that adopted a little boy from an orphanage in the Philippines. The adoptive parents had worked for years to clear all the paperwork and wade through the bureaucratic technicalities, so when word came that the adoption was to be finalized they were jubilant. But when the long-awaited day finally came, and they arrived in Manila after a long plane ride, things didn't go as they had imagined. They expected that they would fall instantly in love with their little boy, that he would adore them, and that they would live happily ever after.

What they experienced at the orphanage was not heartwarming; it was overwhelming. The building smelled of neglect. The children were emotionally distant. And the eighteen-month-old boy that the caretakers brought to them was terrified of them. He cried constantly, inconsolably. On the airplane ride home the new mother tried to feed the toddler, but he refused to eat. She tried to hold him and he pulled away. He wouldn't even make eye contact. She felt completely separated from this boy—physically and emotionally.

The sleeplessness, questions, tears, and frustration continued for weeks while the confused child cried and banged his head on the floor. As she struggled day after exhausting day to comfort him, her thoughts screamed in anguish, *Have we made a terrible mistake? Who is this child?*

One day the boy's eyes met hers and held her gaze for a number of seconds. A tiny spark of trust had emerged. It was a painfully slow process, but little by little a relationship began. One evening she rocked the tiny boy to sleep, listening to him breathe. Her mind asked the old question, *Who is this child?* and a quiet answer murmured back, *He is your son.* Adoption, for her, became a beautiful illustration of grace.

"Even before he made the world, God loved us and chose us in Christ to be holy and without fault in his eyes. God decided in advance to adopt us into his own family by bringing us to himself through Jesus Christ. This is what he wanted to do, and it gave him great pleasure" (Ephesians 1:4-5 NLT).

God purposely pursues his children, pays the price of adoption, feeds them, holds them through sleepless nights, and continues to love them regardless of their actions or rejection, waiting for the moment when acceptance occurs and a relationship begins.

Grace and the Church

Grace, C. S. Lewis famously said, is what distinguishes Christianity from all other faiths. It is fundamental, at the very core of Christianity. The world is ready to experience this grace, which Jesus offers without caveats, footnotes, or prerequisites.

Pastors and leaders can help their churches become places where people in need of grace most readily receive it. They can enable their churches to focus on being loving dispensers of the grace we all have received. They can lead their congregations in the more excellent way.

Untangling attitudes of judgment will be difficult. It will require us to become painfully aware of the unforgiving tones that can creep into sermons, conversation, and e-mails. But when language of hatred stops, healing begins. When the activity of love is seen in the world, people who have felt ostracized by the church will feel the pull of grace.

Whoever we are or whatever we have done, Jesus says, "Come. Follow me." He desires relationship—not mindless, robotic obedience, but relationship with the particular people we are, with our quirks, faults, endearing qualities, and even our muddy history.

Grace also provides a way forward for struggling congregations. Church leaders are searching their souls, as they have been forced to do throughout other painful but ultimately beneficial transitions in history. We are confronting behaviors that have kept the timeless truth of God from being effectively translated into our current culture. When we fully embrace grace, we change everything. Grace, more than anything else, is what we need for the church of this century to move forward.

I learned about this firsthand when I accepted an invitation to become lead pastor of a downtown church. It was a tiny congregation of mostly faithful longtime members. The church had been planted by Swedish immigrants at the end of the nineteenth century and had, over the years, experienced explosive growth. At one time, Sunday worship had brought four thousand or more to the church building.

In the 1950s, coinciding with the national trend toward suburban living, the church began a steady decline, and by the 1980s attendance had dropped dramatically. When I was a candidate for pastor there, the Sunday worship service was attended by an average of 75 to 120 people. There were many wonderful things about this congregation. There was a mix of seniors (individuals who had been attending the church their entire lives) and young people (often the great-great-grandchildren of the original founders). The people cared deeply about one another and truly wanted to serve the city. They had retained a fervent commitment to the message of Jesus Christ. The sanctuary was a beautiful, sacred place that retained its historical reference to a rich past.

With dreams of growing to become a diverse, urban, multigenerational community of faith that could bless the downtown area, we began working together to rethink how to do church in a new time—a process that had occurred numerous times over the church's 130-year history. This loving community had to think about everything: what kind of music would be part of worship, what the bulletins—now called worship guides—would contain and how they would look, ways to communicate with others outside the building, how to partner with neighborhood organizations, whether to do Sunday school or other small group options that gave visitors easier "on ramps" to community participation, and so forth.

The staff was a mix of previous and new that had to be genuine in interactions, sensitive to each individual's point of view, and careful about making knee-jerk decisions. On every level the church needed grace—flowing down the aisles, saturating conversations and attitudes, and emanating from the building. Everyone involved knew the church needed to take its medicine, but it was painful and emotionally charged at times. We needed to keep grace at the center of our conversations.

The congregation sincerely wanted to grow. There was almost bottomless faith that God would do good work here. There was a willingness to examine what new generations of visitors experienced versus what longtime Christians expected. Because of this sweetness of spirit, there were powerful, supernatural experiences occurring every day. The Holy Spirit was at work, bringing new people into the community—not because of the worship service style but because they sensed something going on in this church. Some visitors had left their faith long ago; others happened to wander in because of the proximity of the large hospital campus across the street; some were friends of friends. People tried to hold loosely to their personal preferences. Services mixed historical music with modern pieces. The style of worship was interactive (walking forward for Communion, responsive singing, and spoken Scripture).

It was not a perfect process. It was messy. People tried not to take offense with one another, but sometimes feelings were hurt.

Our journey is to be continued. We don't know exactly where it will lead, but we are seeking transformation, seeking God, and seeking to bless others in radical love, like Jesus.

True Story

One Sunday after worship a senior member of the church approached me. This man was a strong Christian and a volunteer who had spent countless hours serving the congregation over the past four decades. He was very upset. The drums and guitars were too loud. The music had changed to new songs he didn't know or like. He recognized that the service still included some historic hymns, but musicians who wore jeans were playing them. He missed the hymns played on the old organ.

I looked into his eyes and saw the hurt behind the anger. Instead of brushing off the criticisms, I sat with him for a time, uncovering the pain.

I said, "I know it hurts. I *know*. But look at what is happening. New people come into our building and they are intrigued. They feel at home. These people need to hear the message of Jesus Christ, too, and in a way that makes sense in their specific context and culture. Hang on for a while. See what happens."

He didn't leave the conversation kicking up his heels in delight at the changes that were occurring, but we had spoken transparently and respectfully with each other about important issues. We had shared grace.

It is scary to reinvent a church. It means stepping out in faith without a crystal clear picture of the destination. But for any church restart or revitalization, grace is the linchpin. A lack of grace is the deal breaker. Over and over again, we will see how active grace transforms words and people. For any congregation, an overflow of grace will create generosity, patience, and kindness—the gifts of the spirit! God's graciousness creates miracles.

Grace. We need it and we give it. Thus the church rekindles a love affair with people in order to offer expansive hope, fulfillment, peace, and joy to others.

Man and woman
Young and elderly
Friend and curmudgeon
Documented and undocumented worker
Engineer and actor
Mentally ill and mentally profound
African, Swede, Libyan, Pakistani, and Australian
Saint and sinner
Teetotaler and alcoholic
Athlete and couch potato
Gay and straight
Homeless and wealthy
Fit and overweight
Employed and unemployed
Citizen and criminal

These are people God wants to adopt. Let us not be the ones to judge or choose. Let us not stand in the way of God's grace.

Gracious Redeemer, we come to you with overflowing gratitude that you pursue us. Some of us need to be wooed, others need to be embraced, and still others need to be tackled. We are thankful that you do not stop your pursuit. Your grace is always waiting for us. Let us in the church accept the gift of grace from you and grow our relationship with you. Give us the love we need to extend grace to everyone we meet. Help us be about grace, not judgment. Give us the courage to live that grace and convey it. We ask these things in the name and for the sake of Jesus Christ. Amen.

Start Translating

1. Guide your congregation through these personal reflection questions:

Do you view some sins as bigger deterrents to grace than others?

Do you have an opportunity to show more grace to the people around you? To whom? How can you demonstrate grace?

How can you remind yourself daily of *your* need for grace?

2. Host a discussion among your church leaders. In what ways do we deny grace to certain groups of people? Pray together that God will give you opportunities to extend rather than withhold grace.

3. Make a mental list of people—or types of people—you think of as unforgivable. What qualities or sins make them unlovable in your eyes? Now counter that list with how God views these individuals. When you are irritated or troubled by people's actions, how can you seek to understand them and view them as God does?

4. How does your community treat the pimp? The mean girl? The police officer? The bully? The politician? The alcoholic? The country club member? How would Jesus treat those individuals?

5. Invite church leaders and lay leaders to read together *Who Stole My Church? What to Do When the Church You Love Tries to Enter the 21st Century* by Gordon MacDonald. Brainstorm ways to implement new ideas that will open the doors to the broader community, and focus on extending grace to one another during the transitions.

6. As the senior pastor, model grace. Live a life that expresses intentional grace. Be gracious. Express grace—and your own need for grace—in sermons and conversations. Invite staff into this effort. Teach methods of expressing grace when talking through disagreements.

7. Pray for the people in your church who are being pursued by God's grace. Pray with love instead of judgment. It may be useful to become more aware of your own sin so you can accomplish this exercise with humility.

CONCLUSION

It is time to discard old defensiveness, deconstruct unhealthy practices, and guide the church through an exciting and dramatic period of change. The truths Jesus breathed are alive and stronger than ever. We have the ability—and the mandate—to share those realities with a new and receptive audience. Pastors and leaders must grasp the essentials of ministry in our current context and understand their congregations and the many cultures around them in order to construct new bridges to new people.

As we expand our ministry philosophies and skills, adversity will come from both the church and the broader culture. Yet, redefinition, reinvention, and revitalization can happen—even for churches that have suffered devastating decline. Rapid turnaround is possible, but not without cost, collaboration, and new ways of thinking and being.

Most Minnesotans remember Wednesday, August 1, 2007. With rush hour traffic moving slowly through a limited number of lanes across the I-35W bridge over the Mississippi River, the central span of the bridge suddenly collapsed, sending cars, trucks, busses, construction workers, and stunned drivers onto collapsed concrete and the river below. Thirteen people were killed and 145 were injured.

Immediately after the collapse, help came from all around the Minneapolis–Saint Paul metropolitan area. The disaster brought together emergency response personnel, volunteers, charities, and city and county employees. The post-9/11 techniques and technology may have saved lives.

Within only a few days of the collapse, the Minnesota Department of Transportation began planning a replacement bridge. Three months ahead of schedule, on Thursday, September 18, 2008, the new I-35W Saint Anthony Falls Bridge was opened again to traffic. The length of time to complete this project, beginning to end? Twelve months, eighteen days. It was an awe-inspiring accomplishment and a rebuilding effort worthy of acclaim.

The bridge of communication between the church and our society has collapsed. Without that connection, churches will continue to fade. Some sociologists declare the Christian church is a marginalized entity in an increasingly secular American culture. They are right. People today have been inoculated with enough negative Christian religion to create resistance to and even total rejection of the church. This rejection is not necessarily because people are disinterested in Jesus or spiritual matters. Rather, it is because the church has not made a successful transition into the culture and context of this period of time. Some people have been wounded or offended by some segment of broader institutionalized Christianity. The church must again become essential. Ask yourself honestly, "If we and our church disappeared, would anyone in our community even notice?"

Each of us has a part in helping to rebuild the bridge. We must practice Jesus' greatest commandment (Matthew 22:36-40; Luke 10:27): " 'Love the Lord your God with all your heart and with all your soul and with all your strength and with all your mind' [meaning that we love God above dogma, institutions, or self-preservation]; and, 'Love your neighbor as yourself.' " This radical command of Jesus demands that we live sacrificial, empathetic, reconciling, and compassionate lives.

The first followers walked the streets with Jesus, studied with him, prayed with him, and touched him. Living life in the post-resurrection era, Christians became the embodied hands and feet of Jesus to the world around them. Empowered by the Holy Spirit, they fixed their eyes on Jesus and continually led new people to his revolutionary teachings and way of life.

But it was tempting to get sidetracked, even then. Paul was a full-time missionary but had to devote a portion of his attention to advising and admonishing Christians who got off track. "Stay fixed on the One who saved us," he had to continually instruct. "Don't add to the gospel."

As the church of the twenty-first century, we still struggle with distractions that shift our passion away from the rich simplicity of Jesus. Nonessentials can easily prevent us from spending time in spiritual formation, worship, and service to others. Most important, they can get in the way of sharing God's message of grace. So, we must diligently deconstruct all the walls that block people from Jesus Christ. After the debris is removed we then have room for new construction.

The beauty of this new construction is an ancient and future faith design—one that exudes the vibrant Christianity of the early church and aims to highlight the love and grace of Jesus Christ in everything it does. Jesus stands in the center. In that simplicity, the beauty of our faith shines through.

APPENDIX

Suggested Reading

Christian Community

Fuder, John, ed. *A Heart for the City: Effective Ministries to the Urban Community*. Chicago: Moody Press, 1999.

Macintosh, Gary L. *Three Generations: Riding the Waves of Change in Your Church*. Grand Rapids: F. H. Revell, 1995.

Myers, Joseph R. *Organic Community: Creating a Place Where People Naturally Connect*. Grand Rapids: Baker Books, 2007.

Ogden, Greg. *Unfinished Business: Returning the Ministry to the People of God*. Grand Rapids: Zondervan, 2003.

Ott, E. Stanley. *Transform Your Church with Ministry Teams*. Grand Rapids: Eerdmans, 2004.

Leadership

Anderson, Leith. *A Church for the 21st Century: Bringing Change to Your Church to Meet the Challenges of a Changing Society*. Minneapolis: Bethany House, 1992.

Bennis, Warren G., and Robert J. Thomas. *Geeks & Geezers*. Boston: Harvard Business School Press, 2002.

Blackaby, Henry T., and Richard Blackaby. *Spiritual Leadership: Moving People On to God's Agenda*. Nashville: Broadman & Holman, 2001.

Buckingham, Marcus, and Donald O. Clifton. *Now, Discover Your Strengths*. New York: Free Press, 2001.

Cladis, George. *Leading the Team-Based Church*. San Francisco: Jossey-Bass, 1999.

Clinton, Robert. *The Making of a Leader*. Colorado Springs: NavPress, 1988.

Drucker, Peter. *Managing the Non-profit Organization: Principles and Practices*. New York: HarperCollins, 1990.

Gibbs, Eddie. *ChurchNext: Quantum Changes in How We Do Ministry.* Downers Grove, Ill.: InterVarsity Press, 2000.

Goleman, Daniel, Richard Boyzatzis, and Annie McKee. *Primal Leadership: Realizing the Power of Emotional Intelligence.* Boston: Harvard Business School Press, 2002.

Hawkins, Greg, Cally Parkinson, and Eric Arnson. *Reveal: Where Are You?* Barrington, Ill.: Willow Resources, 2007.

MacDonald, Gordon. *Who Stole My Church?* Nashville: Thomas Nelson, 2007.

McNeal, Reggie. *Practicing Greatness: 7 Disciplines of Extraordinary Spiritual Leaders.* San Francisco: Jossey-Bass, 2006.

————. *Revolution in Leadership: Training Apostles for Tomorrow's Church.* Nashville: Abingdon Press, 1998.

Straus, David. *How to Make Collaboration Work: Powerful Ways to Build Consensus, Solve Problems, and Make Decisions.* San Francisco: Berrett-Koehler, 2002.

Webber, Robert. *The Younger Evangelicals: Facing the Challenges of the New World.* Grand Rapids: Baker Books, 2002.

Missional Church and Evangelism

Bass, Diana Butler. *Christianity for the Rest of Us: How the Neighborhood Church Is Transforming the Faith.* San Francisco: HarperSanFrancisco, 2006.

Bosch, David. *Transforming Mission: Paradigm Shifts in Theology of Mission.* Maryknoll, N.Y.: Orbis Books, 1991.

Guder, Darrell, ed. *Missional Church: A Vision for the Sending of the Church in North America.* Grand Rapids: Eerdmans, 1998.

Hunter, James Davison. *To Change the World: The Irony, Tragedy, and Possibility of Christianity in the Late Modern World.* New York: Oxford University Press, 2010.

Hunter, Todd D. *Christianity Beyond Belief: Following Jesus for the Sake of Others.* Downers Grove, Ill.: IVP Books, 2009.

Keifert, Patrick R. *Welcoming the Stranger.* Minneapolis: Fortress Press, 1992.

Kinnaman, David, and Gabe Lyons. *UnChristian: What a New Generation Really Thinks about Christianity . . . and Why It Matters.* Grand Rapids: Baker Books, 2007.

Lewis, Robert, with Rob Wilkins. *The Church of Irresistible Influence.* Grand Rapids: Zondervan, 2001.

Newbigin, Lesslie. *Foolishness to the Greeks: The Gospel and Western Culture*. Grand Rapids: Eerdmans, 1986.

————. *The Gospel in a Pluralist Society*. Grand Rapids: Eerdmans, 1989.

Olson, David T. *The American Church in Crisis*. Grand Rapids: Zondervan, 2008.

Roxburgh, Alan J. *The Missionary Congregation, Leadership, and Liminality*. Harrisburg, Pa.: Trinity Press International, 1997.

Van Gelder, Craig. "How Missiology Can Help Inform the Conversation about the Missional Church in Context." In *The Missional Church in Context*. Edited by Craig Van Gelder. Grand Rapids: Eerdmans, 2007.

Multiculturalism

Deymaz, Mark. *Building a Healthy Multi-ethnic Church*. San Francisco: Jossey-Bass, 2007.

DeYoung, Curtiss Paul. *Reconciliation: Our Greatest Challenge—Our Only Hope*. Valley Forge, Pa.: Judson Press, 1997.

DeYoung, Curtiss Paul, and Michael Emerson. *United by Faith: The Multiracial Congregation as an Answer to the Problem of Race*. New York: Oxford University Press, 2003.

Emerson, Michael, and Christian Smith. *Divided By Faith: Evangelical Religion and the Problem of Race in America*. New York: Oxford University Press, 2000.

Rah, Soong-Chan. *The Next Evangelicalism: Freeing the Church from Western Cultural Captivity*. Downers Grove, Ill.: IVP Books, 2009.

Postmodernism

Bergquist, William. *The Postmodern Organization: Mastering the Art of Irreversible Change*. San Francisco: Jossey-Bass, 1993.

Brafman, Ori, and Rod A. Beckstrom. *The Starfish and the Spider*. New York: Portfolio, 2006.

Frost, Michael. *Exiles: Living Missionally in a Post-Christian Culture*. Peabody, Mass.: Hendrickson, 2006.

Grenz, Stanley J. *A Primer on Postmodernism*. Grand Rapids: Eerdmans, 1996.

Grenz, Stanley J., and John R. Franke. *Beyond Foundationalism: Shaping Theology in a Postmodern Context*. Louisville: Westminster John Knox Press, 1997.

Kimball, Dan. *The Emerging Church: Vintage Christianity for New Generations*. Grand Rapids: Zondervan, 2004.

Miller, Donald E. *Reinventing American Protestantism: Christianity in the New Millennium*. Berkeley: University of California Press, 1997.

Regele, Mike. *Death of the Church*. Grand Rapids: Zondervan, 1995.

Schaller, Lyle E. *Discontinuity and Hope: Radical Change and the Path to the Future*. Nashville: Abingdon Press, 1999.

Sweet, Leonard. *Post-modern Pilgrims: First Century Passion for the 21st Century World*. Nashville: Broadman & Holman, 2000.

Social Justice

Cannon, Mae Elise. *Social Justice Handbook: Small Steps for a Better World*. Downers Grove, Ill.: IVP Books, 2009.

Clawson, Julie. *Everyday Justice: The Global Impact of Our Daily Choices*. Downers Grove, Ill.: IVP Books, 2009.

Morey, Tim. *Embodying Our Faith: Becoming a Living, Sharing, Practicing Church*. Downers Grove, Ill.: IVP Books, 2009.

The Arts

Corbitt, J. Nathan. *The Sound of the Harvest: Music's Mission in Church and Culture*. Grand Rapids: Baker Books, 1998.

Corbitt, J. Nathan, and Vivian Nix-Early. *Taking It to the Streets: Using the Arts to Transform Your Community*. Grand Rapids: Baker Books, 2003.

Fujimura, Makoto. *Refractions: A Journey of Faith, Art, and Culture*. Colorado Springs: NavPress, 2009.

Siedell, Daniel A. *God in the Gallery: A Christian Embrace of Modern Art*. Grand Rapids: Baker Books, 2008.

Worship Design

Basden, Paul, ed. *Exploring the Worship Spectrum: 6 Views*. Grand Rapids: Zondervan, 2004.

Kimball, Dan. *Emerging Worship: Creating Worship Gatherings for New Generations*. Grand Rapids: Zondervan, 2004.

Morganthaler, Sally. *Worship Evangelism: Inviting Unbelievers into the Presence of God*. Grand Rapids: Zondervan, 1995.

Redman, Robb. *The Great Worship Awakening*. San Francisco: Jossey-Bass, 2002.

NOTES

Introduction

1. For statistics and background on the decline of the American church, read David T. Olson's *American Church in Crisis* (Grand Rapids: Zondervan, 2008).

2. Dan Kimball, *They Like Jesus but Not the Church: Insights from Emerging Generations* (Grand Rapids: Zondervan, 2007).

3. David Kinnaman and Gabe Lyons, *UnChristian: What a New Generation Really Thinks about Christianity . . . and Why It Matters* (Grand Rapids: Baker Books, 2007), 24.

4. Ibid., 26.

1. Biblically Inspired: Living the Book with Humility

1. Stanley J. Grenz, *A Primer on Postmodernism* (Grand Rapids: Eerdmans, 1996), 164.

2. Henry Cloud and John Townsend, *How People Grow* (Grand Rapids: Zondervan, 2001), 199–200.

3. Movie Attendance Study, MPAA, 2008.

4. Robert McKee, *Story* (New York: HarperCollins, 1997), 11–12.

2. Prayer Designed: Relying on the Supernatural

1. This and more specific statistics are from research by David T. Olson, *The American Church in Crisis* (Grand Rapids: Zondervan, 2008).

2. Richard Foster, *Prayer: Finding the Heart's True Home* (San Francisco: HarperSanFrancisco, 1992), 7.

3. D. G. Bloesch, "Prayer," in *The Evangelical Dictionary of Theology*, ed. Walter Elwell (Grand Rapids: Baker Books, 1984), 867.

3. Intellectually Informed: Staying Curious

1. Peter Senge, *Leading Learning Organizations* (Cambridge, Mass.: MIT Center for Organizational Learning, 1995), 45.

2. Warren G. Bennis and Robert J. Thomas, *Geeks and Geezers* (Boston: Harvard Business School Press, 2002), 20.

3. Stanley Grenz, *A Primer on Postmodernism* (Grand Rapids: Eerdmans, 1996), 173.

4. Ibid., 169.

5. Mike Regele, *Death of the Church* (Grand Rapids: Zondervan, 1995), 204.

6. Leonard Sweet, *AquaChurch* (Loveland, Colo.: Group, 1989), 238.

7. Erwin McManus, *An Unstoppable Force: Daring to Become the Church That God Has in Mind* (Loveland, Colo.: Group, 2001), 60.

8. Mark A. Noll, *The Scandal of the Evangelical Mind* (Grand Rapids: Eerdmans, 1994), 3.

9. Ibid., 4.
10. Ibid.
11. Ibid.
12. *NIV Study Bible* (Grand Rapids: Zondervan, 1985), 326.
13. Samson was one of the most famous of these judges.
14. P. J. Achtemeier, ed., *Harper's Bible Dictionary* (San Francisco: Harper & Row, 1985), 826.
15. His name actually means "peace" or "peaceable."

4. Communally Formed: Transforming through Relationships

1. Gareth Weldon Icenogle, *Biblical Foundations for Small Group Ministry* (Downers Grove, Ill.: InterVarsity Press, 1994), 131.
2. Dietrich Bonhoeffer, *Life Together* (New York: Harper, 1954), 21.
3. Walt Kallestad, "'Showtime!' No More," LeadershipJournal.net. http://www.christianitytoday.com/le/2008/fall/13.39.html?start=5.
4. *The New Bible Dictionary*, 3rd ed., gives numerous examples of naming in biblical culture and shows how names could signal an event, a status, and even a transformation (Dowers Grove, Ill.: InterVarsity Press, 1996), 810.
5. Gary M. Burge, *John: The NIV Application Commentary* (Grand Rapids: Zondervan, 2000), 76.

5. Collaboratively Led: Rethinking Church Leadership

1. Eddie Gibbs, *In Name Only: Tackling the Problem of Nominal Christianity* (Wheaton, Ill.: BridgePoint, 1994), 243–44.
2. Eddie Gibbs, "From Hierarchical Organizations to Networking Movements: Growing Churches in a Post-Christendom World" (D.Min. class presentation, Fuller Seminary, 2007), MG731.
3. James A. Belasco and Ralph C. Stayer, *Flight of the Buffalo: Soaring to Excellence, Learning to Let Employees Lead* (New York: Warner Books, 1993), 16–18.
4. Donald E. Miller, *Reinventing American Protestantism* (Berkeley: University of California Press, 1997), 138.
5. Peter Drucker, *Managing the Non-profit Organization: Principles and Practices* (New York: HarperCollins, 1990), 222.
6. E. Stanley Ott, *Transform Your Church with Ministry Teams* (Grand Rapids: Eerdmans, 2004), 35.
7. George Cladis, *Leading the Team-Based Church* (San Francisco: Jossey-Bass, 1999), 4.
8. Miroslav Volf, *After Our Likeness: The Church as the Image of the Trinity* (Grand Rapids: Eerdmans, 1998), 33.
9. D. R. W. Wood, ed., *New Bible Dictionary*, 3rd ed. (Downers Grove, Ill.: InterVarsity Press, 1996), 647.
10. David Straus, *How to Make Collaboration Work: Powerful Ways to Build Consensus, Solve Problems, and Make Decisions* (San Francisco: Berrett-Koehler, 2002), 205.

6. Artistically Infused: Joining God's Creative Impulse

1. Gary Thomas, *Sacred Pathways* (Grand Rapids: Zondervan, 1996), 18.
2. David Kinnaman and Gabe Lyons, *UnChristian: What a New Generation Really Thinks about Christianity . . . and Why It Matters* (Grand Rapids: Baker Books, 2007), 125.
3. Paul Engle, *New York Times Book Review*, February 17, 1957.
4. W. H. Auden, "Whitsunday in Kirchstetten," in *Collected Poems*, ed. Edward Mendelson (New York: Modern Library, 2007), 744.
5. J. Nathan Corbitt and Vivian Nix-Early, *Taking It to the Streets: Using the Arts to Transform Your Community* (Grand Rapids: Baker Books, 2003), 75.

7. Mission Minded: Risking Love

1. Craig Van Gelder, "How Missiology Can Help Inform the Conversation about the Missional Church in Context," in *The Missional Church in Context*, ed. Craig Van Gelder (Grand Rapids: Eerdmans, 2007), 38–43.
2. Stanley J. Grenz and John R. Franke, *Beyond Foundationalism: Shaping Theology in a Postmodern Context* (Louisville: Westminster John Knox Press, 1997), 112.
3. Soong-Chan Rah, *The Next Evangelicalism: Freeing the Church from Western Cultural Captivity* (Downers Grove, Ill.: IVP Books, 2009), 162.
4. Rick Rusaw and Eric Swanson, *The Externally Focused Church* (Loveland, Colo.: Group, 2004), 60–61.
5. "Conversion," in *The Evangelical Dictionary of Theology*, ed. Walter A. Elwell (Grand Rapids: Baker Academic, 2007), 296–97.

8. Socially Aware: Seeking Justice for Everyone

1. http://www.merriam-webster.com/netdict/justice.
2. http://dictionary.reference.com/browse/social+justice.
3. Mae Elise Cannon, *Social Justice Handbook: Small Steps for a Better World* (Downers Grove, Ill.: IVP Books, 2009), 21.
4. Ibid., 20.
5. Robert D. Lupton, *Compassion, Justice, and the Christian Life: Rethinking Ministry to the Poor* (Ventura, Calif.: Regal Books, 2007), 22–23.
6. David Kinnaman and Gabe Lyons, *UnChristian: What a New Generation Really Thinks about Christianity . . . and Why It Matters* (Grand Rapids: Baker Books, 2007), 28.
7. Tri Robinson, "Promote Jesus, Not Politics" in ibid., 175–76.

9. Culturally Engaged: Building Bridges of Identification

1. http://www.lausanne.org/all-documents/lop-2.html#2.
2. David T. Olson, *The American Church in Crisis* (Grand Rapids: Zondervan, 2008), 24.
3. Ibid., 50.
4. See Robert Lewis, *The Church of Irresistible Influence* (Grand Rapids: Zondervan, 2001).
5. http://www.internetworldstats.com/stats.htm.

6. http://www.nationmaster.com/graph/med_mob_pho_sub-media-mobile-phone-subscribers&date=1990.

7. http://en.wikipedia.org/wiki/Mobile_phone.

8. Video: A Vision of Students Today. http://www.youtube.com/watch?v=dGCJ46vyR9o.

9. Soong-Chan Rah, *The Next Evangelicalism: Freeing the Church from Western Cultural Captivity* (Downers Grove, Ill.: IVP Books, 2009), 74.

10. http://en.wikipedia.org/wiki/Immigration_to_the_United_States#cite_note-0.

11. "Spiritual Wealth We Can't Miss," interview with Damon Schroeder (audio). http://www.buildingchurchleaders.com/multimedia/audio/spiritual-wealthwecantmiss.html.

12. Rah, *The Next Evangelicalism*, 205.